Playing for the Red Jersey

Dhan a h-uile balach a chluich anns a' gheansaidh dearg.

This book is dedicated to all the players who, over the last 80 years,
have proudly worn the red shirt of Point Football Club.

PLAYING *for* *the* RED JERSEY

A History of Point Football Club

1934 – 2014

POINT FC
1934
Sgioba an Rubha

acair

First published in 2014 by Acair Ltd., An Tosgan, Seaforth Road, Stornoway, Isle of Lewis HS1 2SD

info@acairbooks.com
www.acairbooks.com

Cover & Interior design by Margaret A. MacLeod
Photo of the football boots & Point shirt courtesy of Bryan France & Sandra MacLeod
Photo of the Point Football pitch courtesy of Ross MacLeod

The publishers gratefully acknowledge financial assistance from Point Football Club towards the publication costs of this book.

A CIP catalogue record for this title is available from the British Library

Printed & bound by Hussar Books, Poland

Tha Acair a' faighinn taic bho Bhòrd na Gàidhlig.

ISBN 978-0-86152-567-6

Contents

Acknowlegements

I have to acknowledge the help of many people during the process of writing this book.

Much of this book is based on interviews, memories and reminiscences which emerged from the personal interviews I conducted and from the responses to a questionnaire I prepared. The questionnaire was published in the "Rudhach", the monthly community magazine in Point. I was unsure how people would respond. I should not have worried. The level of response was most gratifying but what was even more significant was the quality of these responses. I have acknowledged all of these people in a separate Appendix to this book. I am so grateful to all of them. They have ensured that this history of Point Football Club is very different indeed from other such accounts of football clubs. I hope that I have done justice to all of them.

Nevertheless, for any historian looking at any aspect of the history of Lewis I have to say that the archives of the Stornoway Gazette still remain the basic source of information. They were absolutely vital and fundamental to my researches. I have relied heavily on reports of matches in the Gazette and the more I read the more I realised why there is still so much loyalty to this local paper. It is, quite frankly, a treasure trove of information, some remembered and some, ashamedly at times, forgotten.

The staff of the Stornoway Library must also be thanked for the gracious way in which they kept supplying me with copies of the Gazette. It would be fair to say that I probably looked at every printed edition of the Gazette from 1933 to the present day. As well as informing me of the history of Point Football Club it also made me more aware of my own history and that of my native island.

Agnes Rennie and her staff at Acair, who have published this book, deserve my gratitude. My special thanks go to Margaret Anne MacLeod who has given so much time and thought to the design of the book. I am indebtited to her.

I want to thank in particular two stalwarts of the club. Ross MacLeod is a former player who played in the 1994 team that won the Highland Amateur Cup. He is also the son of Murdo MacLeod one of the legendary figures in the history of the club. Ross has been hugely helpful to me in checking facts, gathering information and giving me insights into certain aspects of the club. He took an interest in my researches from the very beginning and he has contributed much to this history. I am very grateful to him.

The present Secretary of the club, Iain MacSween, has quite simply given me invaluable support. He has been patient beyond words and he has been able throughout the whole process to look objectively at my many drafts. At times I was well aware of how heavily I was relying on him but he accepted all these demands with good grace and with much humour. This book would not have been written without his help and wise counsel. I owe him much.

My wife, Katrina, has lived with this history of Point Football Club for a long time. She has proof read it in the same meticulous and challenging way that she does with all my written work. It has been made a little more difficult for her given that all her sympathies are with Lochs and with the football team that represents that other special District in Lewis! I thank her, Elizabeth and Niall for everything.

In the end, of course, I take full responsibility for the book and its contents. It has been a great privilege to write it and I want to thank the Point F.C. Committee for inviting me to do so. I hope that the many people who do read it will associate with certain sections of it, nod their heads wisely and acknowledge that this is, indeed, a club of which we can all be proud.

Matthew M MacIver, April 2014

"Days when we played football all day,
nights when we played football by the light of the moon,
returning home across the moor like sweaty ghosts,
the moon a gold football in the sky."

Iain Crichton Smith

Introduction

I was born and brought up in the village of Portnaguran in the district of Point in Lewis. Point is a peninsula situated on the east coast of Lewis and is attached to the rest of the Island by a narrow isthmus called the Braighe. Point, or the Rubha as it is called in Gaelic, consists of 14 villages that make up the District. Because of its geographical situation most of the working population of Point commute to Stornoway, the largest town in the Western Isles. Point has always had a distinctive character of its own and is proudly aware of its own history. The Point Online website is quite unapologetic in describing Point as "a place of beautiful scenery, remarkable history, stunning wildlife and vibrant communities". It is also the home of Point Football Club, an institution very dear to the heart of so many people both at home and abroad.

Our family home is, in fact, the last house in Point. I was a young pupil at Aird Primary School when I first started to watch Point in the 1950s. We did not call it Point Football Club or the Football Team. We just called it Point. It is important to say that because over the years Point FC has been aware of its wider responsibilities. Up until very recently it has been the one consistent organisation that has carried the Point flag very proudly and has been an ambassador for our whole community. It has always been aware of a world beyond the football pitch.

It is within that context that I have written this history of Point Football Club. During the process of writing the book it soon became apparent that so many people wanted to contribute their thoughts that I could not interview them all. I decided to prepare a questionnaire which was publicised in the community newspaper, the "Rudhach". The responses which I received made it so clear to me that many people - players, supporters and interested members of the Point community - wanted to be involved in recording a part of their history which they regarded as important. Much of the book is based, without apology, on these responses. They reveal a loyalty and a pride in an institution which is seen as integral to the development of the District of Point.

That connection is important for me. In the midst of writing about the history of Point F.C. I also wanted to highlight its significance and its importance to the health of the whole district. The football club brought a cohesiveness to Point that other institutions failed to do for the large part of the 20th century. From its formal founding in 1934 it has been a focal point for the community and has made sure that the colour "Red" will always be associated with the District. It has worn that colour proudly over the years.

I also wanted to do something else. I wanted to place this history within a wider context. The Club was born, like many others in the island, at a time of depression and deprivation. It was a desperately difficult time in Lewis following the loss of the "Iolaire" on the first day of January 1919 and the emigrations following the First World War. In the book I have tried to show that football did begin to emerge during this period as a recreation that became increasingly important not just in Stornoway, where it had been established since the beginning of the 20th century, but also in the villages throughout Lewis. Point Football Club was born during that period as were most of the other rural teams in Lewis.

Football in Lewis enjoyed a boom in the years following the end of the Second World War and that public appeal lasted throughout the 1950s and well into the 1960s. As a schoolboy during the 1950s I was a faithful supporter and rarely missed a match. At that time, like so many other teams both in Stornoway and in the rural areas of Lewis, Point played all their games at Goathill Park in Stornoway. Stornoway was a long way away. It was 13 miles away and in a village where there existed not one car that was the equivalent of today's foreign travel. But there was the "team bus" which collected players and supporters alike and then returned after the game. My problem was that I was too young to be allowed to go to these matches on my own. But I had a minder! My mother was quite happy to let me go to the matches if she could be assured that Ian Eric Campbell (Mac Teddy) from the next village, Flesherin, was going. I always gave her that reassurance and Ian Eric did look after me and because of him I watched Point from a very young age.

In the 1960s I actually played several games for Point. As one supporter put it, probably quite correctly, I was "a stuffy right back". I would be the first to admit that I was not very successful but I am proud of the role that other members of my family played in the development of the team in the second half of the century. My brother, Donald Duncan, was an inspirational and industrious centre forward and two of his sons, Matthew and Donald Robert, were players of no mean ability.

After the 1960s came the age of television and the appeal of football in Lewis began to wane. There are, of course, other factors at work. The population of the Islands continued to decline during the 20th century and that brings its own challenges. The Census figure of 1931 shows a population in Point of 3928. In the 2001 Census it had a population of 1675. That is a significant drop in the population and probably gives a fair indication of what has been happening not just in Point but in the Islands as a whole. Added to that, in the latter part of the 20th century, came easy travel to the mainland and the phenomenon of supporters travelling from their own native parts to watch Rangers and Celtic became one that is now well known in the Islands. That is the stage at which Lewis football now exists and the miracle is that it still functions as a healthy community activity. Yet, despite all of these challenges, the game in Lewis still remains competitive and relatively successful. The recent successes of Lewis teams, including Point, in the Highland Amateur Cup bear testimony to that.

Will the game in Lewis survive into the 21st century? I hope it does, not just for the sake of the game itself but because of its importance to the social fabric of the various communities that constitute the Island. Although this book is written from a partisan point of view I hope, nevertheless, that it can also be read as a tribute to all the football clubs in Lewis and especially to those which began as village teams. As organisations these football clubs, sometimes unconsciously, add so much to the cohesiveness of a rural community. In this its 80th year Point Football Club can proudly proclaim that it has done exactly that in the Point community.

When the new Point pitch at Knock was opened in July 2007 at its heart was "Ionad Stoodie". Named after Point's greatest ever player it is a Community Centre which adds another dimension to the concept of a football pitch. These facilities now have the potential to become the centre of the Point community. By adopting Gaelic signage and by creating an obvious Gaelic environment within "Ionad Stoodie" the Club has shown that its roots are in a community that has its own unique language and culture. Within the building itself lies not just a community centre but the very history of the club and, almost inevitably, part of the history of Point itself. Adorning the walls of "Ionad Stoodie" are photographs of Point teams from 1934 onwards. The earliest photograph from the 1930s depicts a team from another world. One of the players has a cigarette in his mouth; another has a cigarette in his hand. Times have certainly changed since then but other things have not. That particular team won the Eilean an Fhraoich Cup in 1934 and thus began the history of Point Football Club. Over the next 80 years it was to become the most successful football club in the island. This is the story of that Club.

Eilean An Fhraoich, 1930s

Foreword

The history of Point Football Club is a glorious one and the recording of it is overdue. Eighty years after the formation of the club is a fortuitous time to address that.

A lot of people care about the legacy left by so many players who have worn the red of Point. One of them, Murdo MacLeod of Broker, contacted me a number of years ago to urge me 'to do something'. I was Secretary of the club and therefore, in a way, responsible for its written record. Murdo suggested I contact Alex Dan Campbell and from there it took off. He contacted all his Point stalwarts to get the ball rolling – John Crichton, Iain Sheordie MacKenzie, Calum Mollie MacLeod, Caillean Beag MacKenzie, Iain Pheaderan Graham. We met in Ionad Stoodie and had a great time. It was clear that these men were determined that the history would be written and they would not take no for an answer but, at the same time, they would not write a book! There were plenty of memories and stories and, from the next generation, Iain Murdo Macaulay and D J Murray were also invaluable with information, team lists and game reports. A lot of the information was available and all it needed, we thought, was someone to bring all that together and make it flow and there's our history book!

The next step was to find a writer, someone with empathy for the place who would do it as a labour of love. As so often happened during the history of this club, it was Murdo from Broker who came up with the solution. It was staring us in the face : Mata, Professor Matthew MacIver CBE, formerly of Number 1 Portnaguran, author of 'My Portnaguran' in the Rubhach, distinguished teacher and head-teacher, former Head of the General Teaching Council of Scotland, Chair of the University of the Highlands and Islands, Professor of the UHI and, most importantly, erstwhile player and life-long Point supporter and thorough gentleman.

Mata took on the task with relish. There is a Gaelic saying – if you want something done ask the busy man – and he had plenty on his plate at the time. There was no persuading required, Mata was up for it! From the outset this was a masterstroke on our part. I attended meetings with the publishers in which it was quite clear that Mata was someone they respected and knew would deliver. I have no doubt that that was the point at which this project became achievable. The first part had been accomplished – we had the best possible writer on our team list and we also had the guys with all the memories and knowledge signed up for the project.

Mata is a historian and his approach to this book is one with which I wholly agree – this was to be a history, not a chronicle. It was not to be a year by year, dry statistical record of team sheets, results, achievements or failures, but was to be a continuous record of a group of young men representing their district as Point Football Club, set in the context of local and national events.

This is a book and a work of history of which I am proud. It records the impact of a sport which now is hugely important in a world-wide commercial sense. However, this is football in its purest form. It is a record of the achievements of a club which has played a significant role in holding a community together through good and bad times.

If anyone deserves the accolade of 'Mr Point' it is Mata. He opened the first Point Agricultural Show, as well as the 10th, he has contributed numerous articles to the Rhudhach and he attends games as an observant supporter whenever his busy schedule allows him. His credentials as a Rhudhach are perfect. And if there is any credit to be claimed by the group that got this project off the ground it is that we got it right when it came to choosing an author.

Iain MacSween, April 2014

Point Football Club Timeline

1933 A team representing the Point district enter their first competition, the **Eilean an Fhraoich Cup**, but go out in the first round.

1934 Point Football Club is formally constituted. The team win their first trophy, the **Eilean an Fhraoich Cup**.

1935 Point win the **Eilean an Fhraoich Cup** again and win the **Lewis Challenge Cup**.

1936 They retain the **Lewis Challenge Cup**.

1937 The **League** is entered and they finish second while also recapturing the **Eilean an Fhraoich Cup**.

1938 Point win the **Lewis Challenge Cup**.

1939 The season is cut short by the outbreak of the Second World War.

1946 Football in Lewis resumes. Point are runners-up in the **League** and winners of the **D'Oyly Carte Cup**.

1947 Winners of the **Tarmod Mor Tankard**.

1951 League Champions for the first time, **D'Oyly Carte Cup** winners.

1952 **League Champions** and **Eilean an Fhraoich Cup** winners.

1953 **Eilean an Fhraoich Cup** won again and **Stornoway Cup** won.

1954 **League Champions** and **Stornoway Cup** retained.

1956 **League Champions** and **Stornoway Cup** winners.

1959 Point do not enter a team in the League but enter the cup competitions.

1960 **Stornoway Cup** winners.

1963 **Stornoway Cup** winners.

1965 **Eilean an Fhraoich Cup** winners.

1966 **Eilean an Fhraoich Cup** winners.

1967 **League Champions** and **Lewis Cup** winners.

1970 **League Champions** and **Eilean an Fhraoich Cup** winners.

1971 **League Champions**

1973 **League Champions, Eilean an Fhraoich Cup** and **Lewis Cup** winners.

1974 **League Champions, Summer Cup** and **Lewis Cup** winners.

1975 **Eilean an Fhraoich Cup** winners.

Home games are now played at the new pitch in Knock.

1977 **League Champions**

1981 League Champions, Lewis Cup, Jock Stein Cup and Acres Boys Club Cup winners.

1983 Eilean an Fhraoich Cup winners, beating Ness 9-5 on aggregate in the first round.

1984 Eilean an Fhraoich Cup and Jock Stein Cup winners.

1985 Eilean an Fhraoich Cup and Jock Stein Cup winners.

1986 Jock Stein Cup and Acres Boys Club Cup winners.

1991 Lewis Cup winners.

1992 Eilean an Fhraoich Cup and Acres Boys Club Cup winners.

1993 League Champions and Jock Stein Cup winners.

1994 Highland Amateur Cup winners.

1995 Lewis Cup winners.

1996 League Champions and Jock Stein Cup winners.

1997 League Champions and Acres Boys Club Cup winners.

1998 League Champions, Eilean an Fhraoich Cup, Jock Stein Cup, Acres Boys Club Cup and Co-op Cup winners.

Visit to *St Etienne* as part of Proisect nan Ealan exchange.

1999 Co-op Cup winners. First of Ceol na Mara fund raising festivals.

2002 League Champions, Eilean an Fhraoich Cup, Acres Boys Club Cup and Co-op Cup winners.

2004 League Champions and Jock Stein Cup winners.

2005 Eilean an Fhraoich Cup and Co-op Cup winners.

2006 Home games played on Tong pitch while Knock is being relaid.

2007 Highland Cup runners-up to Avoch.

New Club facilities are opened at Ionad Stoodie, Knock.

2008 Jock Stein Cup winners.

2009 Hampden Park Football Museum exhibition featuring Point and Back.

Chapter 1

The Beginnings, 1919-1933

Lewis After The First World War

Football came late to the islands especially to Lewis. Scotland's premier club, Queen's Park, was formed in 1867, the Scottish Football Association was formed in 1873 and the Scottish Football League in 1890. It is well into the 20th century, and certainly after the end of the First World War, before we see the growth of football throughout the whole of the Island of Lewis.

The reasons for that state of affairs may not be difficult to find. The First World War itself and subsequent emigrations had taken its toll on Lewis in terms of robbing the island of many young men. In the book "Island Emigrants" Professor Marjory Harper describes the post 1919 islands as an area "beset by economic crisis, with farming and fishing in turmoil, the spectre of famine, special government investigations, financial assistance to emigrants, and active recruitment agents." (1). The sinking of the "Iolaire" on the first day of January 1919 was such a loss that, almost a century later, it is still impossible to assess its real significance both in terms of losing men and sapping morale. What we do know is that the emigrations following the ending of the First World War were devastating in their effects. The "Metagama", the "Marloch" and the "Canada" denuded the island of a whole young generation. It is not surprising, therefore, that it was not until the early 1930s that we see football being organised on a formal basis throughout the island.

That does not mean that football had not reached other islands. There is, for example, a wonderful description of pre – First World War football in South Uist written by Frederick Rea, an Englishman who became Headmaster of Garrynamonie School in the 1890s. It is clear that football was not known to the Islanders at the time. In the book entitled "A School in South Uist" Rea tells of his two brothers arriving from London to visit him in South Uist. He says "they had brought a ball with them on their visit to the island, but the weather had been too wild for football. When the first good day came, the ball was fetched out and blown up in my sitting room, our united efforts with our lungs producing a fairly tight ball. We adjourned to the garden for a game, but a smashed window pane soon made us desist. We then went on the brae in front of the schoolhouse. Sandy espied us and stood there grinning. We invited him to join us; but he had never seen a football before and was nervous." (2)

"Cars were few and the main traffic was horse – driven carts and lorries. Indeed, in those days it was often possible to have a good game of relatively uninterrupted football on the street in front of the Free Church."

Descriptions like that do not exist about the introduction of football to Lewis but we do have references to the development of the game after the First World War. In his book "Lewis in the Passing" Calum Ferguson interviews Allan Campbell who was born in 1922 and he mentions the importance of football for a boy growing up in Stornoway in the late 1920s and early 1930s. Talking of growing up in Kenneth Street he says "Cars were few and the main traffic was horse – driven carts and lorries. Indeed, in those days it was often possible to have a good game of relatively uninterrupted football on the street in front of the Free Church" (3). Later in the interview he returns to the idea of playing "rarely disturbed" football on Kenneth Street, so it must have been a significant part of growing up in Stornoway at that time (4). Admittedly Stornoway Athletic was formed in 1893 and the Stornoway Cup was introduced in 1901. (5). There is evidence to suggest that a league was in

existence in the town of Stornoway from 1903 but, because of the distances involved, there was no opportunity then for rural villages to be part of that league.

That does not mean, of course, that there was no interest in football by this time throughout the various villages. There certainly was and interest was especially strong on the west side of the island where villages like Barvas, Brue and Bragar had established teams. In Carloway, for example, there is evidence that football can be traced back to 1920 "on the initiative of veterans returning from World War 1. Four teams were formed and matches were played on a fairly flat piece of ground at Altan Feirigo in Garenin. Gradually matches against opposition from further afield such as Bragar, Shawbost and Tolstachaolais, were introduced as interest in the sport grew". (6).

In Shawbost it seems that football became established by the early 1930s when "youngsters clubbed together for the purchase of a football which was made of panelled leather enclosing a bladder inflated by means of a cycle pump. The aperture was laced up using a leather thong which was guided into the holes with a specially designed tool". Soon Shawbost was involved in competitive inter-village matches and by the time that the West Side team won the Eilean an Fhraoich Cup in 1938 players from the Shawbost village had progressed to the West Side team. One of their two goals scored in that Final against Point was scored by Donald MacDonald from New Shawbost. (7).

In his book "Around the Peat – Fire" Calum Smith gives perhaps the most detailed description of football in the villages at this time. Calum was born in 1912 and describes the New Year's morning game of football in Laxdale when he was in his final year at Laxdale school. He would have been 12 then so the year is probably 1924. "Two playing areas were used, known as the "little pitch" and the "big pitch". Then he

Point Football Team and Supporters – The photograph was taken on the 5th May, 1947 on an outing to Ness.

Back row – Pringle, Shader; Kenny John Dobac (Shader); Unknown (maybe Ian Grant?); Sandy Mor, Garrabost; Domhall Choinnich Bhig, Garrabost; Murdo Graham (Sissy), Garrabost; Moban, Garrabost; Kenny Starry, Shader.

Front row – Dodo Allan Handy (Scrubie), Shader; Stoodie, Garrabost; Kenny Alistair an Fortair, Garrabost; Commence, Shader; Fiscan, Shader; Dod, Garrabost; Alex Dan Archie, Shader.

adds "To call either a pitch was an act of faith" (8). I think we all know what he means.

Later in the book he tells us that in May, 1928, just before he was 16 he was offered his first trial game for the Nicolson's First Eleven team. That gives some indication of the development of football after the war of 1914-18. Between then and his demob after the Second World War Calum Smith tells us that that he played for the school (the Nicolson Institute), Unionists, Sandwick, Caledonia and the Rovers. (9).

Certainly by the time that Point Football Club play their first game in 1933 there is plenty of evidence that football in the rural villages of Lewis has developed significantly. That is also the case in Point. We know that football was played by boys in the villages at this time. The most eloquent expression we have of these days come from the novelist and poet Iain Crichton Smith, born in 1928, who writes of his boyhood in Bayble:

"Days when we played football all day, nights when we played football by the light of the moon, returning home across the moor like sweaty ghosts, the moon a gold football in the sky". (10).

> "Point were beaten 2-0 by Back in the first round and so began a rivalry which is "the longest-lasting and the deepest – rooted in Hebridean football.""

We also know that village football by this time was organised on a more formal basis. The official history of Back Football Club indicates that "The first inter village game in Point was a nil-nil draw between Aird and Sheshader. Other teams playing in Point in 1933 were Flesherin, Shader and Garrabost" (11).

The likelihood, however is that there were probably teams in almost all the villages. Angus Munro (Unna) from Knock, born in 1923 and a stalwart of the immediate post war Point team, told me that he remembered teams from Melbost, Aignish, Swordale, Knock, Aird and Garrabost. In 1934 and 1935, for example, we can find references to newly formed teams like Lochs playing friendly games against Lower Bayble as well as official games against Point. (12).

It was into this world of village teams that Point Football Club was born. As a team representing the District of Point they played their first game in the inaugural competition for the Eilean an Fhraoich Cup on the 16th August, 1933. The introduction of the Eilean an Fhraoich Cup to Lewis football is well documented. In March 1933 the Glasgow Lewis and Harris Association announced it was donating a cup for the rural teams in Lewis and that event became the very foundation of a formal structure for football in Lewis. The West Side Football Association, the pioneers of rural football in Lewis, were asked to draw up the rules and organise the competition. Lewis was divided into eight areas - Ness, West Side, Carloway, Uig, Point, Back, North Lochs and South Lochs – and only players living or born in the area could play in the competition. These rules have been somewhat circumvented over the years but essentially the Eilean an Fhraoich Cup still retains its attraction as a tournament solely for rural teams in Lewis. (13).

Seven teams entered that first competition, among them a team from Point. The others were Ness, West Side, Carloway, Uig, Tarbert and Back. I have found no evidence to suggest that this team which entered the 1933 competition was a formal, fully constituted Point team which had been established by a committee or by some other formal means. My guess is that an ad hoc Point team was brought together to accept the invitation that had come from the West Side Association. There was enough village football at the time to enable a Point Select to be chosen quite quickly. This is what I think happened. Some might argue that this alone would indicate that Point F.C. dates back to 1933. My own view is that it would be safer to assume that the team of 1934 is probably the first official Point team. As I explain in the next Chapter, there is strong circumstantial evidence to point to 1934 but I accept that there is no hard evidence to prove this.

> "Ta, 's fhada gu faigh iad
> an ath Mhinistear bhoinne."
> ("It will be a long time before they
> get the next Minister from us")"

There was some form of poetic justice in the fact that the inaugural Eilean an Fhraoich Cup was won by the West Side who beat Uig over two legs in the Final. Point were beaten 2-0 by Back in the first round and so began a rivalry which is "the longest–lasting and the deepest – rooted in Hebridean football". In an article specially written for an Exhibition on Football Rivalries in Scotland at Hampden Park in 2009, Iain MacSween, the present Secretary of the Club, has written at length about this local rivalry which, in football terms, goes back to the 1930s but whose real origins are to be found "in the water that separates the two districts – Broad Bay or Loch a Tuath. At one time this stretch of water, 10 miles long and 4 miles wide, provided many families on its edges with their livelihood. It was teeming with cod, haddock, ling and whiting and fishing boats crewed by men from villages on both sides vied with each other for bragging rights". The fishing declined but the "bragging" continued on the football field and it is testimony to the long-running success of both teams that it still stands out as the keenest of rivalries in football in the Western Isles. (14).

In 1947, for example, a Minister from Point moved to take charge of the congregation at Back Free Church. In the summer of that year Point lost 2-0 to Back in a hotly disputed game. The Gazette of the 27th June carries a quote from a Point cailleach reportedly saying "Ta, 's fhada gu faigh iad an ath Mhinistear bhoinne". ("It will be a long time before they get the next Minister from us"). Apocryphal as the story might be, it illustrates the friendly rivalry that has always existed. The old cailleach, had she lived, would have been delighted to know that the latest Ministerial acquisition in Point has in fact moved the other way across Broad Bay.

That first game against Back signified that something new was about to begin in the District of Point. The inaugural Eilean an Fhraoich Cup itself heralded the beginnings of organised football throughout the Island of Lewis and with that came a new era in the history of the Island. It was not surprising that this was happening. Football was by this time a huge social phenomenon in Scotland. In April of 1933, for example, 134,170 fans turned up at Hampden to watch Scotland beat England 2-1. Little did anyone realise that other events in that year were to dictate so much more. In January of 1933 Adolf Hitler was elected Chancellor of Germany and by that time both Benito Mussolini and Joseph Stalin were in power in Italy and Russia respectively. Another new era was about to begin in Europe that was to influence the history of the world at large. But that was for later years; in the meantime a few years of peace lay ahead and football in Lewis was to enter a phase of development which was to determine its shape and structure until the present day.

Chapter 2
The Foundations

A Peaceful Interlude, 1934-39

It has been impossible to identify the exact date when Point Football Club was officially constituted. Nevertheless it is clear that following their entry into the Eilean an Fhraoich Cup in 1933 there are very definite moves towards forming a Point team in the next year. The Stornoway Gazette of the 18th May, 1934 carries an interesting report of a game played between Lower Bayble and a Point Select. The Select team includes players from the whole District – from Garrabost, Aird, Sheshader, Aignish, Melbost, Shader and Upper Bayble – and although there is no indication in the Report that this is the real beginnings of Point F.C. I suspect it is. The Eilean an Fhroaich Cup which they were about to enter was played in the autumn and it looks as if this was an attempt at the beginning of the summer to look at players from the various village teams in order to choose a District team. Certainly the game attracted interest and the Gazette reports that the spectators "travelled from all over the district". The game incidentally ended as a 3-3 draw and the star player was A.J.Maclean from Aird.

Further proof that a team was being developed comes in another Gazette report of 14th September 1934 when a Point team played the School team from the Nicolson. The game was played on the "Melbost machair" and "the crowds rolled up in their hundreds to see how their own braw lads would shape up against their redoubtable opponents". We must remember that the School had an established team by this time and Point did well to draw with their "redoubtable opponents". Among the players in the Point team that night were Calum Sgarry, Alasdair Archie, Dolly a Bhodaich and John Angie Dollag. My own strong view is that, taken with the rogue entry into the 1933 Eilean an Fhraoich Cup, these were the stepping stones towards the formation of the official Point team that was entered for the 1934 Cup.

Further impetus probably came from the fact that, following the success of the inaugural competition in 1933, the responsibility for running the competition moved from the West Side Football Association to the Eilean an Fhraoich Cup Committee and this particular committee was well populated by Rubhachs. Its first President was John MacSween and Donald MacKenzie was the Secretary/Treasurer. (15). John MacSween was born and brought up in Garrabost and became a legendary Headmaster of Aird School which he served from 1929 to 1951. He is also acknowledged as the architect of Lews Castle College, becoming its first Principal when it opened its doors to students in 1953. Donald MacKenzie from Shader (Dolly a Bhodaich) later became the Headmaster of Lionel School in Ness in the 1950s and 1960s. He was actually a member of the 1934 team. These were strong forces at work ensuring that Point would indeed have an official football team. It was no surprise, therefore, that Point Football Club formally started its official history with its entry into the Eilean an Fhraoich Cup competition in 1934.

It was a successful entry. Point won the competition and that began a wonderful history of commitment and success that has lasted to the present day. In the final Point beat West Side over two legs. Interestingly Point was still using the "Melbost machair" as their home ground and after winning 2-0 at Melbost they held West Side to a 1-1 draw on the 10th September 1934 at Barvas to win their first trophy. Their goals in the first leg were scored by Calum "Sgarry" MacRae and Dolly MacKenzie and the latter also scored in the second leg.

The contemporary reports of the two games are interesting insofar as they seem to suggest that West Side were not at their best and had they been they would have beaten Point. That is reasonable given that Point were a new team and West Side were the team that had initiated village football in Lewis and had organised the first Eilean an Fhraoich Cup competition. Nevertheless, Point won convincingly and the Gazette report of the 19th October, 1934, was forced to admit that "the Point team as whole appeared a very smart and lively lot". In the

first game the star of the team seems to have been their young goalkeeper from Shader, J.A. Murray (John Angie Dollag), a "young schoolboy who played with great coolness and confidence". In the second leg their star was the centre half, M. MacKenzie from Branahuie "whose judicious generalship both in defence and attack was a great factor in the success of the team".

The cup was presented to the Point Captain, J. MacLeod, at a social gathering in Bragar immediately following the game. It was presented by John MacSween from Aird who commented in his speech that "he was very glad to see so many of his former pupils showing that they were taking an active interest in football and sport generally". Much more significantly, he seemed to appreciate the importance of what was happening in terms of Lewis football in general. He recognised that the Eilean an Fhraoich Cup had succeeded in "spreading the game to all parts of the Island" with the "result that football in rural Lewis had made extraordinary progress".

The Gazette report acknowledges that the Cup victory was received both by Point players and supporters alike "with admirable restraint". The Captain, J. MacLeod, said that he was proud of the team and Mr Donald MacKenzie, President of Point Football Club, spoke in similar terms. Up until now references to Donald MacKenzie have described him as the Secretary/Treasurer of the Eilean an Fhraoich Cup competition. The fact that he is now addressed as the President of Point Football Club suggests that, by now, Point F.C. is a formal, constituted football club. That is the strongest piece of evidence we have that the Club was formally constituted in 1934. In fact, it is the only written evidence that seems to exist which gives us any indication of the founding of the club. That is why I believe that 1934 should be seen as the founding date for Point Football Club.

The success of 1934 was continued throughout the rest of that decade. The Eilean an Fhraoich Cup was retained in 1935

Point Team – Eilean An Fhraoich 1934 or '37

Back row – D W MacKenzie, K Munro, C Murray, M MacKenzie, J A Murray, M MacDonald, A J MacAskill, D MacKenzie, M MacLeod, J MacKenzie

Front row – M MacRae, J MacIver, J MacLeod, A MacLeod, A MacDonald

when Uig were beaten 3-1 in the Final. Dolly MacKenzie and Calum "Sgarry" MacRae were again among the scorers, as was Alex MacLeod. Another new cup again for rural teams, the Lewis Challenge Cup, was also won in 1935. The interesting fact about this game was that it was played in front of a record crowd of 1500 spectators at Goathill Park and brought in revenues of £17, nearly double the existing record. (16). The success of the Eilean an Fhraoich Cup had a profound effect on the developing standards of football in the villages. In 1936 a Town v Country match was organised where the Country team was selected by the Eilean an Fhraoich Committee. The Stornoway Gazette of the 11th September 1936 could say that "Football in rural Lewis has made astonishing strides within the past twelve months". Four Point players were chosen for that game – J.A. MacRae (Goalkeeper), A.J. Maclean (Right Back), K. MacLeod (Left Half) and J. MacLeod (Inside left). Although the Country team lost that game 2-1 it was clear that football in the villages had come of age.

> "Football in rural Lewis has made astonishing strides within the past twelve months."

In the following year, 1937, came the single most important development in Lewis football when the Lewis League was formed and rural teams entered the League that had been established in Stornoway for some time. In 1934 the Stornoway Football League consisted of six teams. They were Athletic, Caledonian, Rovers, Sandwick, School and Unionists. By 1937 only Athletic, Rovers and School remained to represent the town of Stornoway. Together with Back, Ness, West Side and Lochs, Point entered the new League and finished a respectable second, two points behind the Rovers. Ironically Rovers, having won the first ever Lewis League, never won it

again and withdrew from competitions after the 1990 season. (17). On the other hand Point and their rural colleagues had embarked on a journey that was to define their future histories.

Success in the Eilean an Fhraoich Cup continued with a win over two legs against Lochs. They won 3-0 in both games and their scorers were Alistair "Archie" MacDonald and Murdo Dan MacLeod (2) in the first leg; and Alex MacLeod (2) and Kenneth MacLeod in the second leg. As far as the Stornoway Gazette was concerned the only incident of note in that second leg happened outwith the pitch. In its edition of the 17th September 1937 it reports that "the second half began with a determined Lochs attack, in the course of which Nicolson missed the goal but scored a bull on a horse grazing quietly behind the goals. When interviewed the unfortunate animal was somewhat incoherent, but a vigorous protest from him to the SFA is anticipated".

In 1938, the last year that competitive football was played in Lewis until after the end of the Second World War, Point again had a relatively successful season. They won the Buchanan Cup beating Lochs 3-1 in the replay and a disputed goal in that game led to an animated correspondence in the Gazette. They reached the Final of the Eilean an Fhraoich Cup only to be beaten in a replay by West Side who won by 2-1. The scorer for Point was Torquil MacLeod. Perhaps it was appropriate that the West Side did indeed win that Final of 1938 because they had done so much during the 1930s to introduce organised football to the rural parts of Lewis and consequently to the whole island. One of the players in that West Side team, Donald MacDonald, was present at the Final in 2013 when West Side was again successful. He gives a fascinating insight into the differences between the football of the late 1930s and the football of the early 21st century. Quoted in the Gazette of 8th August 2013 he says "I saw so many differences to the game itself from our day. Players today are of a much higher standard for a variety of reasons. The ball for one, especially in the wet, as our ball was much heavier. Today's boots are like slippers in comparison which in turn allows players to be faster than we were. I think the style of football too is different now and we never passed the ball backwards. If we had we would hear shouts from the touchline saying we were going the wrong way".

That was the last competition until 1947 when peace had been restored in Europe. For the duration of the 1939-45 War the Eilean an Fhraoich Cup remained on display at Shawbost School, a reminder of a decade which had seen the spread of football throughout the island and the birth of most of today's football teams in Lewis including Point. (18). The debt that football in Lewis owes to the Eilean an Fhraoich Cup and the vision of those who initiated it is immense. Arguably what it did was to bring villages and communities together in a way that had not been done since the Evangelical movements of the early 19th century. The effect of football was as profound as that in Lewis.

> "The debt that football in Lewis owes to the Eilean an Fhraoich Cup and the vision of those who initiated it is immense."

But football, like normal life, was now abandoned as the world drifted towards the Second World War. The 1930s had seen the rise of the Dictators and the increasing spread of Fascism in Europe. That political situation was reflected in football at international level. In the year that Point was formed and won its first trophy, the World Cup was won by an emergent Fascist country, Italy, and symbolically the country that was beaten in the Final was Czechoslovakia, a country that was to disappear later in the decade under the onslaught of Hitler's army. Four years later, in 1938 in France, history was to repeat

itself when yet again Italy won the World Cup against another country, Hungary, that was to suffer at the hands of the Fascist Dictators.

There would, however, be no more World Cups until 1950. On the 3rd September 1939 the British Prime Minister, Neville Chamberlain, announced that Great Britain was at war with Germany. Normal life was suspended in Britain as it was in most countries in the world. Not surprisingly, planned football programmes were suspended yet football itself continued in a sporadic kind of way throughout the war years in Britain. Off the field enthusiastic volunteers kept it going and on the field ordinary servicemen found themselves at times playing in the same teams as established International players. Despite all the problems inherent in coping with a war, the game of football itself grew in stature during these years, playing a huge part in maintaining morale. When peace returned football's popularity was enormous and there is no surprise in the fact that organised football in Lewis returned immediately after the Second World War ended in 1945.

Chapter 3
The Post War World

Football Returns, 1945-60

"A six year truce ended on Christmas Day when Back and Point resumed the football argument where the late spot of unpleasantness with the Third Reich interrupted it."

Under the heading "Peace Rejoicings" the Stornoway Gazette carried a report on the formal ending of the Second World War. In its edition of Friday the 17th August 1945 it wrote "In many hundreds of homes in Lewis and Harris people sat late by their wireless sets on Tuesday night to hear Mr Attlee's historic announcement – 'Japan has today surrendered. The last of our enemies is laid low.'" Hundreds of young men returned from the war but some, unfortunately, did not. Among them was John Angie "Dollag" Murray from Shader, one of the young Point stars of the 1930s and the goalkeeper in the team that won that famous Eilean an Fhraoich Cup in 1934. He left Glasgow University in 1941 and was drowned on his very first voyage during the Second World War. (19). Many of those who did return were physically fit and some of them had played football at a senior level in the Forces. Partly for these reasons the post Second World War era was to herald possibly the healthiest period of football that the Island of Lewis has experienced.

Almost inevitably the first formal football match to welcome the new era was between the old rivals, Point and Back. As the Stornoway Gazette of the 4th January 1946 unambiguously and wryly put it:

"A six year truce ended on Christmas Day when Back and Point resumed the football argument where the late spot of unpleasantness with the Third Reich interrupted it.

Goathill Park was sodden, but in reasonably good condition for the occasion: the weather was cold and dry: the crowd cold, but, in the main, not so dry."

The festive crowd was treated to a glut of goals, the match ending in a 6–6 draw. What is just as interesting is the analysis of the two teams and their style of play which, according to the Gazette reporter, had not changed since pre–war days.

Lewis Select which beat Ross County 7-5 in 1946. This photograph was taken on Christmas Day.
Front row, 2nd from left – John Murdo "Stoodie" MacKay

Back were quick in the tackle and pass, playing "flat out" for 90 minutes. Point were more deliberate and studious and put much more work on the ball. Whether this is a true reflection of the two styles is difficult to assess but what is certain is that it was Back who prevailed at the end of that first post war season. The title was decided on the very last day of the season on the 21st August 1946 when the last game was played at the Airport. Again the weather conditions were not favourable. "The Airport pitch was largely under water, and declared dangerous for play by the referee, but, to avoid disappointing the big crowd, the players decided to risk injury, pneumonia or drowning". It was not a wise decision by Point; they lost 5-0.

It is important to point out that rain was a specially difficult challenge to footballers at this time in the late 1940s and 1950s. A hugely evocative and delightful description of Lewis football in the 1950s is given by Norman MacArthur, "Am Brot", who was no mean footballer himself. He played for both Carloway and the famous School team of the 1950s with whom he won two League medals. Entitled "Memories of Carloway Football Club" he describes a world unknown to the present generation but well known to many of us.

"The ball was leather and laced and particularly on a wet muddy pitch became very heavy compared to the party balloon type of the present day. Passing the ball sideways or backwards was a foreign concept rarely seen as was a pass to a centre forward with his "toin" (backside) to the opposing goal.

The playing system in the 1950s was the W formation where you had a three man defence of two agile backs and a commanding centre half, two half back ball winners who fed two powerfully engine inside forwards, fast wingers who hugged the touchlines and a centre forward whose job was simply to score goals". (20).

But despite all these challenges football had resumed. The next 15 years following the end of the war were to be relatively successful for Point and, overall, it was a time when Lewis football as a whole was hugely attractive to spectators and highly successful when pitted against teams from the mainland. On Christmas Day 1946, for example, a Lewis Select took on Ross County and beat them 7–5. Five of the Select's goals were scored by the Point player, John Murdo "Stoodie" MacKay from Garrabost, who was to become a post war Lewis legend.

Arguably the best player Lewis has ever produced, and certainly regarded as Point's greatest player, "Stoodie" had trained with Northampton Town and Mansfield Town during the war and had actually played for Mansfield Town in the season 1945 – 46. (21). The coaching he had received among professionals, allied to his physique and speed of thought, made him a formidable centre forward. Prematurely balding and sturdy in build, defenders could be forgiven for underestimating him – until the game started. Notable for his heading ability and the power of his shot it is little wonder that the Point club facilities are named in his honour.

His son, Angus, who has become a Point stalwart himself, remembers how his father was fondly remembered in many homes throughout Point. "As a young boy helping deliver the milk around Point on my father's milk round I soon became aware of his football prowess as I was regularly regaled with past Point FC exploits in the households of Biodan, Tarmod Tomsh, Hoddan, Coinneach Starry and Pringle". He was also highly regarded throughout the island football fraternity where his exploits in the Lewis Select teams were well documented. In an article about the Lewis Select in 1954 the football correspondent of the Gazette, under the title "The Great Stoodie", could say "I wonder where League officials and fans would look for a replacement for Stoodie MacKay? Is there any Lewis football fan who hasn't cheered for Stoodie at one time or another? In every bus, pub or on street corners, whenever fans congregate the name of Stoodie invariably crops up. Time after time, I've heard the comment, "If it wasn't for Stoodie". "Stoodie won the game, etc, etc". And significantly, he's always been an automatic choice for the Select".

Point Team, 1947-48
Back row – J MacDonald, M MacRae, N MacMillan, A Munro, A MacDonald, M MacDonald
Front row – D MacSween, J Campbell, J M MacKay, M D MacLeod, K MacDonald

Stoodie's great abilities were also recognised among players of his own era. Unna Munro regarded him as the best player he had seen – someone who could score from any angle but also someone who had built such a reputation for himself that "they were out for him". He remembers one night in Ness when "Stoodie" was carried off and Unna himself was "afraid for him". The "Biodan", Murdo MacLeod from Broker, was also quite unequivocal in his judgement "In my opinion he was the best" although I was interested that both rated a contemporary, Alex MacLennan from Back, as also being an outstanding footballer. George MacAskill (Snr) who played for Point between 1952 and 1964 recalls that one of his most outstanding memories revolved around "Stoodie". He remembers playing for a Lewis Select against Inverness Caledonian on 3rd July 1954. Caley had a big centre half named MacFadyen who kept shouting all through the game "keep your eye on the big fellow!" He meant "Stoodie". Although the Lewis Select lost 5–2 that day "Stoodie" inevitably scored one of the Select's goals.

It should not, however, be assumed that this was a one man team. It certainly was not. That particular Lewis Select team contained not just "Stoodie" and George MacAskill but also one of the other great Point servants, John "Hoddan" MacDonald from Bayble. Hoddan was a physically imposing centre half who possessed enormous leadership qualities on the pitch and is rightly remembered as one of the "Greats" of Lewis football. The Point teams of this era were sprinkled with names of players who could have graced any football pitch; names like Pringle MacAulay, Norman "Tarmod Tomsh" MacDonald, Malcolm "Molly" MacLeod, Kenny "Starry" MacDonald, Willie John Campbell, "Taman" MacRae, Murdo "Fushie" MacIver and John "Ston" Campbell.

The 1950s, therefore, saw the emergence of one of the great Point teams. This, after all, was the team that won the League in 1951, 1952, 1954 and 1956. The Eilean an Fhraoich Cup was won in 1952 and 1953; the Stornoway Cup was won in 1953, 1954 and 1956; and the D'Oyle Carte Cup was won in 1951.

This was the team that could attract six bus loads of supporters to the 1952 Eilean an Fhraoich Cup Final when they beat Back 4-2; a feat they repeated in 1953 when they beat their old rivals again by 4-3.

By the beginning of the 1956 season the Gazette could report that "Hoddan" was "not so dominating as in his younger, speedier days" yet in the same edition it was reporting that George MacAskill was "wonderful to watch. If there is a better winger in these Islands he's still to appear." (Gazette. Friday May 4, 1956.) Other new players included Angus "Angan" MacKenzie from Flesherin, a wonderfully talented and tenacious left–back. In other words, a new generation of players was emerging to take over from those who had formed the team in the years immediately following 1945. There were even rumours that "Stoodie" would not appear again in a red shirt. But appear he did and helped the team to yet another League title. That particular League win was against stiff opposition from the School and United. It was well earned. The Gazette of the 16th July, 1956, acknowledged that fact when it wrote "They have won by the typical Point virtue of never letting up, no matter how the game might be going". The icing on the cake was winning the Stornoway Cup when they beat United 3-0.

For "Stoodie" it was his last season and there was something symbolic about that. Lewis football was dominated for the next four years by a strong United side which in 1957 went through the League programme without dropping a point. For Point F.C. a worrying time emerged. It was not difficult to explain. Boys went off to the Merchant Navy to earn their living and were not at home at the times when the team needed them. Others went to places like Glasgow where there was work in the industrial centres of the Scotland of the 1950s. Matters were not just difficult in Point, they were also difficult in Lewis football as a whole. The Stornoway Gazette of March 10, 1959 could report that only five out of ten members turned up for the Annual General Meeting of the Stornoway Football Association when they were supposed to organise the Lewis

League, Stornoway Cup & Eilean an Fhraoich Cup winners, 1952
Back row – A J MacLean, W J Campbell, N MacRae, C MacLeod, I MacIver, K J MacKay, J West, D MacDonald
Front row – G MacAskill, P MacAulay, M MacIver, J MacDonald, J M MacKay, N MacDonald, N MacKenzie

League & Stornoway Cup winners, 1956

Back row – M MacLeod, D Nicolson, N MacRae, J MacDonald, M MacLeod, C MacLeod, J Graham, K MacDonald, D MacDonald

Front row – G MacAskill, A Graham, J M MacKay, B Whitelaw, N MacDonald, N MacKenzie

League for the coming season. After a long and sometimes bitter meeting they finally agreed on what was to happen.

Sadly Point was not going to be part of what they had agreed. In April 1959 it was announced that Point would not be competing in the League. This is how the Gazette reported the news on April 28, 1959 "There is one team less in the League this year – Point. Owing to the lack of interest the team has had to be disbanded. When the club held their annual general meeting a few months ago only one person turned up". It brought to a sad end the era that had seen triumphs on the field and the development of a group of players who, at times, saw the game of football as exactly that – just a game.

In this post war era, and especially in the 1950s, the rule of law on the park was sometimes stretched a bit. On one occasion a penalty was awarded to Point against the RAF team and the ball was solemnly placed on the spot. Biodan purposefully stepped back to take a run at the ball. One of the more spirited members of the team, perhaps getting impatient with procedures, raced past the Biodan and walloped the ball into the net. Re-take and an early bath for Tarmod Tomsh! Stoodie once stopped in his run–up to take a penalty, the goalie dived and everyone fell about laughing while the ball remained on the spot. "Goal kick" the referee decided.

> "I came home from sailing and there wasn't a Point team in the League. The Club was in debt up to its ears."

All of that, however, happened in the good times and the events of 1959 threatened to bring to an end the very existence of a football team which, for almost 30 years, had brought pride to a whole district. It is without a doubt the lowest point in the history of this proud football team. As the Biodan put it to me "I came home from sailing and there wasn't a Point team in the

League. The Club was in debt up to its ears". But the team did not stop playing. That was important. A small committee kept it going and a Point team was fielded in the Cup competitions and performed remarkably well. In the Eilean an Fhraoich Cup, for example, they reached the semi – final only to be knocked out by the West Side. The Phoenix had indeed risen from the proverbial ashes and the next fifteen years were to prove that the Rubhachs were made of pretty stern stuff.

Kenny John Murray and Coinneach "Starry" MacDonald

Point Team, 1957
Back row – D Nicolson, N MacRae, M MacLeod, N MacKenzie, I Graham, J MacDonald, K MacDonald, N MacAulay
Front row – I Crichton, G MacAskill, W J Campbell, J P MacKay, W Munro

Point Team, 1963
Back row – A D MacMillan, P J MacLean, N MacKenzie, A Allison*, I Graham, I A Campbell, N MacDonald, M MacLeod
Front row – I Crichton, N J MacDonald, C MacKenzie, A MacIver, A D Campbell*regular goalie P MacRitchie missing from photo

Chapter 4
Rebuilding for the Future

The 1960s

That Point survived as a football team after the events of 1959 was due to the efforts of certain individuals. Two supporters in particular ensured that Point would have a team, if not in the League, at least in the Cup competitions during the 1959 season. They were Alex Dan MacMillan, a business man from Shader who owned the Crown Hotel in Stornoway, and Murdo MacLeod, the Biodan, from Broker. Murdo is quite unequivocal in giving Alex Dan much of the credit for the survival of the team although the truth of the matter is that he underplays his own contribution. The fact is that by the end of the decade the Stornoway Gazette could report on September 14, 1968 that "Point's successes are in no small way due to the efforts of Murdo MacLeod who has, single handed, given a great deal of time and energy in keeping the team in the forefront".

This was a decade when the Scottish standing in the game was never higher. In 1967 Celtic became the first British club to win the European Cup beating Inter Milan in Lisbon and Rangers reached the Final of the European Cup Winners' Cup in the same year only to lose to Bayern Munich. In Lewis it was not an easy time for clubs like Point given that an exceptional Athletic team began to dominate island football. Added to that was the fact that football in Lewis was also generally in a healthy state. Those of us who attended many games during this time remember teams like the RAF (The Lily Whites) who played in an all white strip, the School team who played most of their games early in the season because of school holidays and Stornoway Builders. They all contributed to Island football at that time. The Gazette of 25 January, 1964 reported that the annual meeting of the Lewis Football Association had confirmed that attendances at matches had been increasing throughout the 1963 season. Not only that but the Chairman, Mr Alistair MacDonald, commented that standards which had been falling in the 1950s were now rising.

Point F.C. was also back in business. It re-entered the League in 1960 and given the challenges that faced them, the season was remarkably successful. The team finished a respectable 5th place ending the season with a resounding 7-4 win against Athletic. Sometimes they had to rely on players who were not from the District simply to field a team. The best example of that was Alistair Morrison (Alistair Stobbie) from Lochs who had played professional football with Greenock Morton. Fielding some of these non – Point players was not without its difficulties. In August, for example, they had to replay a game against Carloway because they had played three players not officially released by other clubs.

There were other controversial moments and games. The most memorable was a game against Back at Coll in July 1961. This is how Malcolm Flower, the present Chairman of the Club, describes it." This was my first trip to an away game with the team on the bus (BJS 337). The bus collected the players at the Neptune and as what appeared to be a usual occurrence did not leave on time, due to one or two stragglers having a final Lucozade! The players changed in the bus and the game kicked off about ten minutes late. After 20 minutes or so Back took the lead controversially, a Point player was sent off and all this eventually resulted in the Point team walking off the park. I could not believe what was happening. Before we could draw breath we were back in town. It was my first away match with the team."

Trouble had actually arisen at a previous match when Back fielded three visitors to the island who were not eligible to play. They were three professional players one of whom was the Scottish Internationalist, Ian Ure, who played for Dundee and Arsenal. The others were Bobby Adamson and John Baxter both professional players. Point were beaten 2-0 in that game and protested to the Football Association. When the Association met to consider the Point protest they were not quorate and so a decision was not made! But Back themselves conceded they were wrong and agreed to pay Point's travelling expenses for a replay at Coll. The only problem was that a local referee, Kenneth Graham from Coll, took charge of a game where a neutral might have been wiser. From contemporary reports of the game in the Gazette of 18 July 1961 it appears that "the standard of refereeing on this occasion was no different from many rural matches". That, however, did not suffice. The referee awarded a doubtful goal to Back, sent the Point Captain, Malcolm (Molly) MacLeod, off for refusing to give his name and the whole Point team walked off the park. In the Gazette of 1 August 1961 we learn that Point were censured, the score of 3-2 for Back was allowed to stand and Molly MacLeod was suspended for 14 days.

Nevertheless, despite all the challenges, it was a remarkably successful decade for Point. That first season of 1960 - a season that had promised so little - brought its own highlight with the winning of the Stornoway Cup when they handsomely beat Back 5-0. The Gazette report of 26 August 1960 was fulsome in its praise for the Point performance that night. "Point were superior man for man and as a team even further. Their football is the best seen in the Island for a number of years, and it is impossible to pick out individual stars, so well does every member play."

Perhaps that was not surprising when one considers some of the players who played that night. In goal was Alistair Morrison (Alistair Stobbie) and with him were Rubhachs of the quality of John Graham (Iain Pheatarain), Angus "Angan" MacKenzie, John Crichton and George MacAskill. It is not a surprise to learn that George MacAskill, despite all the successes that he had wearing the Point colours, regards this game as one of his outstanding memories. "We were 5-0 up against Back after 15 minutes; don't ask the final score – I can't remember!!". The old rivalry was alive and well. And after all these years George remembered the score perfectly.

Stornoway Cup Winners, 1963 – This was the last time this Cup was ever played

Back row – M MacLeod, A J MacRae, A MacLeod, P MacRitchie, N MacRae, I A Campbell, I MacRitchie

Front row – M Nicholson, I Crichton, C MacKenzie, I A MacRae, A D Campbell

Point Team, 1969

Back row – A MacLeod, D MacDonald, D MacKay, I MacRae, W MacDonald, K MacLeod, N MacDonald, K MacSween, I Graham

Front row – W Jefferson, S Martin, J Crichton, K J Campbell, D D MacIver, A D Campbell

In 1963 the Stornoway Cup was again won. After a 5-2 victory against United and a 3-1 win over the RAF in the semi final they beat Shawbost 4-2 in the Final. The goals were scored by Colin MacKenzie (2) and Murdo Nicolson (2). There is a photograph of the 1963 team showing both Alex Dan MacMillan and Murdo MacLeod standing proudly with the players. It is actually one of the happiest team photographs that exist in the Point F.C. archive. That might have something to do with the fact the team was by then quietly putting down roots again and were developing players who would themselves become Point heroes.

They were good enough to win the Eilean an Fhraoich Cup in 1965 when in heavy conditions at Goathill they comprehensively beat Lochs 7-0 and so avenged their 2-1 defeat earlier in the season in the Spring Cup Final. Five of their goals that night were scored by Kenny "Bobbans" MacDonald who usually played for Athletic and the other two were scored by Colin MacKenzie. The Eilean an Fhraoich Cup was retained in 1966, the Lewis Cup was won in 1967 when they beat Athletic 2-1 in the final and in the same year Point won their first league title since 1956.

From the beginning of the 1967 season it looked as if Point had the potential to be successful. The Gazette of 13 May, 1967 asked if Point were going to be "the new soccer supremos of Lewis football" after they had beaten the reigning champions, Athletic, 3-0. There were, of course, glitches; it would not have been the Point of the 1960s had there not been. The match against West Side in April was abandoned ten minutes from the end when the Point team walked off. They insisted that the light was too bad to continue - contesting the West Side goal which they claimed had gone over the bar and not under it!

As it turned out the winning of the League was a very close run thing. In effect, Lochs lost the League by losing 2-1 to Builders in the dying seconds of their final game. It ought to be said that this was a fine Lochs team with Kenny MacSween, that beautifully talented footballer, playing his first full season for the team. Point took advantage of Lochs' late slip by beating Builders 3-0 to win the League which at one stage could just as easily have been won by Athletic. It was, according to the Gazette, "one of the best soccer seasons on the island for quite a number of years".

The fact that by 1967 Point had won the League spoke volumes for the work that had gone on behind the scenes to recover from the events of 1959. There is no doubt that despite the difficulties that the team had faced at the beginning of the decade a very successful rebuilding process had taken place. Youngsters had accepted responsibility. The team of 1963, for example, contained emerging talents like Norman "Snosh" MacDonald, Norman John MacDonald and Alex Dan Campbell. These were names who were going to play significant roles in future successes. But the experienced players were also there. This was the era of players like Murdo Nicolson (Murdo Shockan) from Garrabost, Colin "Bayble" MacKenzie, Iain "Sheordie" MacKenzie from Bayble and Calum Finlayson from Garrabost. They were players who were always going to be successful and who were going to influence their young team mates. That could certainly be said of their star player, Calum Finlayson.

Calum Finlayson was one of the classiest footballers who ever played in Lewis. He was an elegant mid field player who had great vision and could command a game. Other players responded to his athletic and skilful presence in the middle of the park. It was no great surprise that Calum had a successful career in Scottish Junior Football with Bonnyrigg Rose to whom he was farmed out from Hibs. Had he not broken his leg (twice) while playing with Bonnyrigg he would have gone on to greater football heights. That is the accepted view of those players who played with him in the 1960s. Donald Duncan MacIver describes him as "the best player I ever played with. He was a different type of player – fitter and on another level".

Malcolm Flower simply says that Calum Finlayson was "surely one of the great Point and Lewis footballers".

But Calum Finlayson was not on his own. Young players like Iain Alec MacRae and Willie "Frogie" MacDonald were coming through from the Junior ranks and this side also had players of the calibre of these two great servants to the Club, John Graham (Iain Pheatarain) playing at the back and John Crichton (Iain Uilleam), playing in the middle of the park. These two simply epitomised everything that Point Football Club stands for. They were born leaders on the park. When they both served the Club as Manager they showed the same leadership qualities on the touchline.

It is quite indicative of his enormous enthusiasm for the team that one of John Crichton's outstanding memories of his career was when he was dropped! "We were tying for the League with United" John recalls, "and needed to beat the West Side to play in the League decider against United. Playing against the West Side I scored all four goals to beat them 4-0. On the evening of the League decider our manager decided to drop me and introduced two boys who had not played all season. Needless to say they drew 0-0. That was the only time that I was dropped and I nearly caused World War Three in the dressing room!" That is exactly what you would have expected from Iain Uilleam – total commitment.

Other players like Iain "Sheordie" MacKenzie also brought quality to the side. Iain came up through the football ranks. As a schoolboy he played in both the Kemnay and Ladywell Cups, won the Roma Cup with Bayble in 1957 and captained the Lewis School Select. He was without doubt the outstanding schoolboy footballer of his generation in Lewis. He came into the team in the 1961 season and played until the mid 1970s. He then became a football administrator but has never lost his sense of loyalty to Point F.C. He regards the team of the 1960s as exceptional and mentions in particular Ian "Growdie" MacLeod from Knock as one of the key members of the team.

He is also aware that some marvellous players like James "Topsy" MacDonald from Flesherin did not get a regular game. "That's how good a team we had".

When they won the League in 1967 the Stornoway Gazette carried a photograph on its front page of the team with their Manager, the ubiquitous Murdo MacLeod, under the caption "Champions of Lewis". But in an almost unconscious way they were also champions of Point itself. No one should underestimate what the club achieved for the whole community of Point in the 1960s. As a team, following the events of 1959, they had faced their own challenges in rebuilding their football future. This they had done with steely determination and not a little skill.

In reality, however, they were more than football champions. The 1960s was a difficult time for the District of Point when a religious controversy threatened to split the community irrevocably. The football team was the only institution that carried the united aspirations and hopes of the District during these difficult times. Not only did they do that but they also initiated, during the 1960s, the whole process of rebuilding a community for the future. They proudly and unequivocally represented the whole community playing together and working together. The red jersey became the symbol of a community striving to live together and brought self confidence back to a District which desperately needed it. Let no one be in any doubt about the importance and influence of the football team in that troubled decade. What it did remains one of the most significant achievements of the club in its eighty year history.

Point team, 1960's

Back row – W Jefferson, J Graham, P MacRitchie, I MacRae, N MacDonald, D MacKenzie

Front row – T MacKenzie, I Crichton, C MacKenzie, K MacDonald, A D Campbell

Calum Finlayson, Willie Jefferson, Tom MacKenzie

Chapter 5
The Move to Knock

The Process

Point, like so many other teams in Lewis, played virtually all their home games at Goathill Park in Stornoway. At the very beginning in the 1930s we know that they played on what was called by the Stornoway Gazette the "Melbost machair" and immediately following the war it was called the Airport Pitch. But Goathill was the word that became part of the football vocabulary. It was, and remains, a respected and well loved part of the fabric of Lewis football. As Unna put it "'S e Cnoc nan Gobhar Wembley" – "Goathill was Wembley to us". A player of the 1970s, Donald Duncan MacIver, simply said that "Goathill was our home".

But the search for a pitch in Point started very early on. On the 24th November 1950 a Feu Charter was signed by the Stornoway Trust giving feu disposition to the office bearers and members of the Point Athletic Association (Point Football Club). (22). The feu disposition refers to a piece of land "forming part of the Common Pasture of Knock and Swordale and extending to three acres and seven hundred and seventeen thousandths or decimal parts of an acre". So, the Club effectively took possession of a plot of land amounting to just under four acres. That is the land which now houses our football pitch. What the legal papers also verify is that the Point pitch is in Knock and not in Garrabost. It is easy to see why this mistake can be made. The original Title Deeds mention that the land is situated opposite 17 New Garrabost but goes on to make it clear that the plot of land itself is contained within the common pasture of Knock and Swordale. Interestingly by the time that the Club, then referred to as the Point Recreation Club, was granted permission in 1985 by the Stornoway Trust to build a pavilion on the land the reference to 17 New Garrabost still remained. Nevertheless, both legal documents make it quite clear that Point's pitch is in Knock. That has always been the case and the media, and indeed many people, are wrong in insisting that it is in Garrabost. It is in Knock.

It is interesting to note who the Point Office Bearers were in 1950. They are identified in the legal papers as Murdo MacLeod, 7 Aignish, President; John Murdo MacMillan, M.A., 42 Nicolson Road; John MacMillan, 1 Shulishader, Secretary and Treasurer; Norman MacLeod, The Schoolhouse, Knock; Malcolm Roderick MacDonald, 38 Geileir, Bayble; Alexander Graham, 1 New Garrabost; Neil Macaulay, 6 Shulishader; Donald MacKenzie, Post Office, Portnaguran; and Roderick MacKenzie, 22 Upper Bayble.

> "Bha an dàrna duine eòlach air an duin' eile. Football did that for us. It brought people together..."

Many of these are well known names in Point. Some like John Murdo MacMillan and Norman MacLeod epitomised the important role that school teachers and Head Masters played in the development of Lewis football; others like Alexander Graham from Garrabost became legendary and faithful supporters of the club. There is further interest in the fact that one of the Trustees of the Stornoway Trust is John MacLeod, 16 Portvoller, Seonaidh Aonghais Uilleim, who was a significant business man in Point in the middle of the 20th century. In general terms, therefore, these Office Bearers are exactly what you would have expected – a good cross section of the Point community working hard to ensure that the local football team would have a home in its native District.

In the passing it is interesting to note that when I interviewed Angus Munro (Unna) he emphasised, without any prompting from me, how important the team was as a way of bringing people together at that time. He was particularly strong in emphasising the influence of teachers and Head Masters. He mentioned people like Donald MacDonald (Bayble), Murdo MacLeod, (also Bayble) and Alex Maclean, (Aird). George MacAskill (Snr) made the same point to me strongly when he wrote. "I owe a big 'thank you' to Mr A.J. Maclean Headmaster at Aird School and Mr Donald 'Doul' MacDonald Head Master at Bayble School who were in charge of the team at the time". Unna saw this contribution as being of social importance in a small community. As he put it "Bha an dàrna duine eòlach air an duin' eile. Football did that for us. It brought people together and we had concerts to raise money not just in Point but in other parts of Lewis as well". The same point was made by the Biodan who insisted that from 1951 "I was always arranging concerts, sales of work, etc. That continued for the next 50 years believe it or not!"

Yet, despite these attempts to raise money for the team and for the new football pitch, there was a long road to travel before the Club actually began to play at Knock. That did not come until 1975 and "was the result of a huge community effort with many people chipping in with whatever they could, from tradesmen building the changing rooms to small boys clearing the stones off the playing surface. By today's standards the pitch may have had a home-made feel to it but it served the community very well over the next thirty years". (23).

Norrie MacDonald (Norrie Tomsh) tells the most lovely story of that community effort that made the pitch at Knock a reality. Norrie played for Point in the 1970s and 80s and when the pitch was being constructed was in charge of one of the Youth teams in Point. He wrote "The year after I started playing for Point there was a concerted effort to provide a home pitch for the 'sgire'. A piece of land was acquired and there was a sponsored stone-picking to clear the land in order to build the original pitch. All the youth of the area were there, as there was a case of Donnie Soval's lemonade on offer for the first team to get to 20 buckets of stones. My team was tied on 19 with a mob from Bayble when someone had a bright idea. We 'bought' a full bucket of rocks off a team languishing behind for two bottles of Orange. You had to be pretty devious growing up in Aird!" But he finishes by saying with a note of pride "the new park was tremendous".

Yet in terms of the Club's facilities the best was still to come. On the 28th October 1985 the Stornoway Trust granted permission to the Trustees of the Point Recreation Club to build "a suitable building or buildings" on the site at Knock. (24). The Trustees at the time are, like their predecessors in 1950, all well known Rudhachs. The President was Murdo MacLeod (Broker), the Chairman was Iain MacIver MacKenzie (Stornoway but originally from Bayble), the Secretary was Murdo Donald MacLeod (Shader but originally from Portnaguran) and the Treasurer was Iain Morrison from Garrabost.

The Title Deeds of 1985 are, in effect, the green light for proceeding with what is now known as "Ionad Stoodie" and with that also came a new pitch. It was 22 years before that actually happened. Much effort was made in the intervening years to ensure that not just Point FC but the whole Point community would have recreation facilities that would serve the District. In the 1990s the Point Sport and Recreation Association had been formed to achieve that very aim. The members' commitment and fund raising efforts were rewarded when the new facilities were opened on the 16th July 2007. On a wet and miserable evening Point FC met a Rangers FC U-19 squad to open the pitch formally. On the night the main guests of honour were two former Rangers' Internationalists, John Greig and Ronnie Mackinnon.

Perhaps more significantly was the fact that two local stalwarts were also guests of honour. They were the indomitable Murdo MacLeod (Biodan Narrow) and the former Head Master at Aird, Alasdair MacDonald. Murdo's contribution to Point FC has been colossal. A native of Broker he is simply an integral part of the history of the Club both as a player, manager, trustee, office bearer and lifelong supporter. Alasdair laboured for many years at Aird School both in the cause of education and the development of football among the young. He served as a member of the Island Football Association and was one of the original supporters who started the process that lead to the development of the pitch at Knock. Acknowledging these two was so important. It was an official recognition of the contribution of individuals over the years. Murdo and Alasdair would be the first to admit that they were representing so many others who had worked for such a long time to ensure that the Club now had a permanent home in Point.

All these volunteers had, of course, achieved more than a home for a football club. They had brought facilities to Point which were open to the whole community. The Chairman of the Point Sport and Recreation Association, Matt Bruce, said in his Introduction to the Souvenir Programme produced specially for the night "that the facilities we now have will bring more local interest in sport and physical exercise". The building, he said, "is there for all, not just footballers!" That philosophy encapsulates what the Club had been doing since its formation in 1934. It has always served its community and when it finally came home to a permanent pitch in Point it is greatly to its credit that it did not forget its history and it remembered the legacy it had inherited.

League Cup, Lewis Cup and Eilean an Fhraoich Cup Winners, 1973

Back row – M MacLeod, D MacKay, J Crichton, I MacRae, W Jefferson, J M MacDonald, I MacKenzie

Middle row – (unknown), (unknown), C Nicolson, N MacAskill, (unknown), J Graham

Front row – D MacDonald, A MacKay, D D MacIver, A MacAskill, M A MacSween

League Cup, Lewis Cup & Summer Cup Winners, 1974
Back row – M MacMillan, A MacKay, I MacKenzie, N MacAskill, I MacRae, A MacAskill, J Graham
Front row – I Crichton, A Campbell, W Jefferson, D MacKay, M MacLeod, M MacSween

Chapter 6
The Move To Knock

The Effects

In the wider world, the year 1970 saw Donald Stewart beat the sitting MP, Malcolm K MacMillan, to win a historic election in the Western Isles. Malcolm K MacMillan had been the Labour MP for 35 years but lost by 762 votes to the SNP candidate Donald Stewart. It heralded the beginning of a new era not just in the politics of the Western Isles but in Scotland as a whole. From now on the SNP Party was to become an increasingly important player in the world of politics in the UK. In the Western Isles this decade also saw the birth of Comhairle nan Eilean with the Local Government reforms of 1975. For the first time in modern history the Outer Hebrides from Lewis and Harris in the North to Eriskay and Barra in the South were brought together. That was to change forever the way that the Islands were to be administered. In the political world, therefore, there was a new feeling abroad and in football, both in Scotland and in Lewis, another era was also beginning.

The Scottish International team qualified for the later stages of the World Cup in West Germany in 1974 and under the management of Willie Ormond and the leadership of Billy Bremner performed well. They were now the ninth best international side in the world and that was no mean achievement for a country that had spent years in the football wilderness. There were some similarities in terms of improvement with a Point team that was itself developing as a formidable force in Lewis football.

The Point team of the 1970s has been rightly seen as one of the strongest ever to represent the District. The knowledge that they were going to move to their own ground in Point, and the move itself, had immediate effects. Point became the dominant team in Lewis for most of the 1970s. During that decade they won the League five times, the Eilean an Fhraoich Cup three times and the Lewis Cup twice. As the programme for the opening of the new pitch in 2007 puts it "The old campaigners from the sixties had been strengthened by new recruits like Norman "Buck" MacAskill, Donaulay MacKay, Murdo "Turra" MacSween, "Fred" MacRae, Angus "Fushie" MacIver, Donald Duncan MacIver, Alexander MacKay, Willie Jefferson, Alasdair MacLeod and others". The "others" included talented youngsters like Kenny John "Punka" Campbell and Coinneach Chalum MacLeod both from Portnaguran. The strength of the young talent available can be gauged by the fact that in 1970 a youngster of 17, Donald Duncan MacIver, had already captained the Lewis Youth Select and had won a League medal as well as an Eilean an Fhraoich Cup medal.

They won the League in 1970 with a consistency that the Gazette described as "devastating". In June their 6–1 defeat of Back was being reported as the "best performance by a Point team in recent years – the eleven men in the side blended together in perfect cohesion. Their performance was faultless with every member of the team playing their parts to perfection, and to single out individuals for special mention is a difficult task. However, if one has to do this, centre – half I. A. MacRae, centre forward K. Campbell and outside - left A.D. Campbell are the ones that come to mind". In addition to the League they beat Lochs 1-0 to win the Eilean an Fhraoich Cup.

Another League championship followed in 1971. In fact, by May of that season, the Gazette was predicting that "Point are real championship contenders. They are a good all-round team, sound in defence, razor-sharp up front and spurred on in mid-field by the promptings of J. Crichton". The title was won with a 2-1 win against United and further titles followed in 1973, 1974 and 1977. It was ironic that in season 1975 when "their own pitch is ready for the season and the finishing touches are being put to the new changing rooms beside the pitch" they did not win the League. It was won by a strong Back team. Playing on their new home pitch Point had started off as favourites in 1975 but they had a poor season by their own standards. Yet they had a strong team analysed by the Gazette in these terms "The Point team's strength has been their defence – they have been well served in goal by MacAskill

and MacDonald. The half back line of Crichton, MacRae and Jefferson seem to be like good whisky, improving with age".

In the season of Homecoming they left their best performance for the Eilean an Fhraoich Cup Final when they beat Back 4-2. As the Gazette put it "Donaulay MacKay, the indomitable captain, who has led the Point team to many cup successes in recent years was proud of his team's performance. He and his team mates thoroughly deserved the Eilean an Fhraoich Cup". But there was an ominous last paragraph in the Gazette report. "Point will have to look to their junior players for any future success as several of this year's team have already played their best games".

The pessimism seemed to be misplaced. Point came back to win the League in 1977 in resounding style under the leadership of their manager Willie Jefferson. As far as players like Donald John Murray were concerned they were managed well. "The most tactically aware manager I played for was Willie Jefferson. He was really astute and could spot things in an instant and change things round accordingly". This was the season when no games were played at Goathill Park which was ploughed up and reseeded. In the past that would have had a profound effect on Point but not anymore. They began their campaign with an impressive 4-2 win against Back in Coll and ended with a 2-1 win against Harris in a title decider.

A wonderfully descriptive account of that game was sent to me by Donald John Murray from Shader. "One of my outstanding memories is of the final game of the 1977 season against Harris. Harris only needed to draw while Point had to win to secure the League title. "Walrus" Morrison (who was later to star for Point) cynically took out our star player "Turra" MacSween in the early stages of the game and that set the tone for the rest of the game. Harris took the lead and then had what seemed a good goal disallowed. Point equalised and went on to lead 2-1.

"In the final moments of the game "Walrus" Morrison hit a tremendous shot from just inside the Point half and the ball rattled off the bar. Colin Campbell (who played for Hibs in

Point Team, 1977

Back row – W Jefferson, A MacAskill, D MacKenzie, D MacKay, J Crichton, M MacDonald, A Dunlop, D MacDonald, J MacRae, M MacMillan

Front row – I MacKenzie, M I MacRae, E MacKenzie, A Campbell, M A MacSween, K I MacLeod

the Scottish Cup Final two years later) picked up the rebound and with only the keeper to beat blasted the ball over the bar. The game finished shortly afterwards and Point under Willie Jefferson had won the League.

"Three sides of the pitch had been roped off prior to the game and in my memory it's the biggest crowd I can remember at a home Point game. The cars that night were as far down as Claypark, in the Lower Bayble Road and up past Seaview.

"I went round and collected the gate money with "Murdo Townie" in a plastic bag and when counted it totalled £89.00. This was at a time when people used to throw 10p and 20p coins into the bag so it gives an indication of the crowd that night."

Donald John's recollections are confirmed by the press report of the game. At least 550 people attended the game according to the Gazette of 10 September, 1977 and "the road out of Garrabost was blocked for over thirty minutes. What an astonishing end to the senior football season". In its analysis of the game the Gazette was hugely appreciative of the efforts of one of the Point stalwarts. "Several of the Point players were also outstanding – none more so than John Crichton. At almost thirty-eight years of age he is still as fit and as efficient as he was when he started playing way back in 1956 – or was it 1955".

John Crichton's generation and the team of the 1970s had set enormously high standards for succeeding teams to equal. Some would argue that the next successful Point team – the team of 1981 – not only equalled these standards but surpassed them. Certainly there is a strong argument that the Point team of 1981 was exceptional. What they achieved in one season is unparalleled. They won all their eighteen league games with the loss of only eleven goals for the whole season while scoring seventy. They won the Lewis Cup, the Jock Stein Cup and the Acres Boys' Club Cup. The only trophy to elude them was the Eilean an Fhraoich Cup. The slight crumb of comfort to be taken from the loss of the latter was that one of their players, Angus "Charlton" Murray, played for Tolsta who won the trophy. That

gave "Charlton" the distinction of being the only player in Lewis football to have won all the medals available in the one season.

The fact that "Charlton" did play for Tolsta illustrates the tensions and loyalties that exist in an Island community when it comes to a competition like the Eilean an Fhraoich Cup. "Charlton" had dual nationality! He belonged to Point but he also belonged to Tolsta. This is how he put it himself. "My brother and I were Swordale boys and although our parents were from Tolsta and we moved there in 1970, we retained an affiliation with Point, and Swordale in particular. So I was flattered to be asked by Iain Crichton to play for Point at the end of season '79. He was a great motivator and not the kind of guy you wanted to disappoint. Much later, of course, he became my father in law!" That, however, did not stop "Charlton" playing for Tolsta in the Eilean an Fhraoich Cup in 1981 and carving for himself a slice of Lewis football history.

Despite not winning the Eilean an Fhraoich Cup there is no doubt that this was one of the great Point teams. The League success of 1981 was followed by wins in the Eilean an

	P	W	D	L	F	A	Pts
Point	18	18	0	0	70	11	36
Ness	16	10	2	4	68	26	22
Rovers	18	8	3	7	43	34	19
Back	18	7	5	6	30	35	19
Carloway	18	8	2	8	49	45	18
Athletic	17	9	0	8	34	29	18
Harris	18	7	0	11	31	56	14
United	16	5	2	9	22	45	12
Lochs	15	5	1	9	29	33	11
Tolsta	17	1	1	15	12	74	3

The League Table, 1981

League Cup, Jock Stein Cup, Lewis Cup & ABC Cup Winners, 1981
Back row – J Crichton, A Murray, I Morrison, A Campbell, N MacAskill, N MacDonald, A MacLeod, D J Murray, D MacKay, M MacMillan
Front row – D MacDonald, I MacAulay, I MacDonald, N J MacDonald, N MacLeod, R MacKay

Cup Winners Display, 1981 – League, Acres Boys Club, Jock Stein & Lewis Cup Winners

L to R – I MacKenzie, J Crichton, N MacAskill, A Murray, A Campbell, N MacDonald, N MacLeod, D J Murray, N J MacDonald, F Stewart, D MacDonald, I MacAulay, I MacDonald, D MacKay, A MacLeod, R MacKay, I Morrison, M MacLeod

Eilean an Fhraoich Winners, 1983

Back row – D MacDonald, J Wood, R MacKay, N MacAskill, D MacDonald, I D Murray, A Clinton, N J MacDonald, M MacMillan

Front row – I Morrison, N MacDonald, I Finlayson, A MacLeod, A MacKay, I MacAulay

ABC Cup Winners, 1986

Back row – D MacDonald, K MacDonald, N MacAskill, M MacAulay, C MacKenzie, A MacLeod, R MacKay, M MacMilllan

Front row – I Finlayson, I MacAulay, G MacDonald, N MacDonald, N MacLeod, M MacDonald

Fhraoich Cup in 1983, 1984 and 1985. They had players of undoubted quality - Norman "Buck" MacAskill, Norman John MacDonald, Norrie "Tomsh" MacDonald, Robert MacKay, John Angus "Fluffy" Murray, Malcolm "Ollie" MacLeod, Alasdair MacLeod, Iain "Fairy" Macaulay, John Murdo MacDonald, Iain "Walrus" Morrison, Alasdair Campbell, Angus "Charlton" Murray, Donnie Steven MacDonald, Finlay Stewart and Donaulay MacKay who broke his leg during that season.

The 1981 team had, in "Charlton's" words, "some excellent players; an excellent keeper in the late "Buck" MacAskill; steel at the back from the likes of Robert; the late "Ollie" MacLeod (best header of a ball I have seen in any amateur league) and Donnie Stevie; power and subtlety in midfield from Walrus and Alasdair "Gaelic" respectively; and youth and pace from relative youngsters such as Norrie "Tomsh", Alasdair Campbell (very quick) and Fairy." But the best player of his generation was the "imperious Norman John MacDonald. Although probably past his best, he was an intelligent player, very confident and led the line well. It was actually an education to play with him".

Certainly the players themselves felt that they were involved in something that was special. As "Charlton" puts it "1981 was a memorable year for Point F.C. – League and three cups and no defeats. We also played a Caley team under the lights at Telford Street and won 7-5, although we might have had a "ringer" or two. Quite a number of the Point team also played for the Select that beat Skye 7-0 that year at Coll Machair. While the '81 team was made up of older guys and younger guys – about half and half – the crack and the dynamic was really good. Post match celebrations were usually in the Carlton which was slightly problematic for myself as I was barred at the time! There were also a lot of characters in and around the team at the time and a hard core support".

Later on that hard core bunch of supporters became affectionately known as the "Grumblies". They were supporters like the Biodan, Alasdair "Creachan" Graham , the Peasdon,

Alastair Shonnie, Pringle, Tarmod Tomsh, Willie "Jeff" Jefferson, Donald "Freush" MacDonald, Shewan, Donnie "Dodo" Wilson, Willie John Teddy and Shonny Fhionnlaigh. There were more. Essentially they were the Point F.C. groupies.

Perhaps the original of the lifelong Point supporters and a stalwart of the "Grumblies" was Neil "Peasdon" Macaulay. He was never a good footballer but he grew up in Shader in the company of village boys who were to star for Point in the 1940s and 50s – his brother Pringle, who stood out with his fair hair and elegant movement, his next door neighbour Kenny John Murray, a hard tackling and skilful half-back and the immaculate Kenny "Starry" MacDonald. They were all merchant seamen and away from home for long periods but these three were automatic choices for the team when available. Neil was a seaman all his working life and spent his later working years on the Calmac ferries on various routes on the west coast. He was a faithful committee member for many years but he also performed other tasks to keep the club afloat, such as selling raffles at the gate. An abiding memory of him is his quick march across the park to tell the Grumblies in the old corrugated shed the winning number after the half-time draw for the half-bottle. He was there when the Highland Amateur Cup was won and it was clear how much it meant to him after a lifetime supporting the club.

The "Grumblies" stayed loyal for many years after this "annus mirabilis" and were regular supporters at all the home games – grumbling constantly but immensely proud of their own team. They became hugely inspirational in their own idiosyncratic way, gathered in later years in the same place at the right hand corner of the stand for each game. They were the stereotypical "critical friends" ready to shout constructive criticism but the first to acknowledge achievement. As Ross MacLeod puts it "If you were winning you were not winning by enough; if you were losing you were losing by too much". Their loyalty to Point was unconditional and their expectations were enormous.

Jock Stein Cup Winners, 1986

Back row – R MacKay, I MacRae, A MacLeod, A MacKay, N MacAskill, M MacAulay (hidden), G MacDonald, D MacDonald, N MacLeod

Front row – I Frater, M MacDonald, I MacAulay, (Shona MacKenzie with cup), N MacDonald, I Finlayson

The loyalty and ambition of the players who were not regulars in the 1981 team were also impressive. Those players who were not in the first team were desperate to play so that they could take part in the process. Iver MacDonald was such a player. "I was on the periphery of the team, a handy, keen go-to if anyone didn't turn up. There were whispers before each game as to who was working late, had an injury or for some other reason couldn't make it. As a super-sub, as John Crichton used to call me to massage my ego, I was aware of my fragile status in the team. Norman John MacDonald used to come home specially for big games and finals. He wore a long leather trench coat and carried his boots in one hand with a kit bag over the other shoulder. One more in the queue before me".

It was difficult for players like Iver to play second fiddle to Norman John. Yet they stayed totally committed. Despite what he calls his fragile status Iver takes pride in what was achieved. "I have two girls who know the Point pitch as a local landmark when we go home, but they have no idea of what went on that summer of '81. Someone should write a song about it". Donald John Murray was in a similar position and felt exactly the same. One of his abiding memories is "the sheer jubilation after the final game of the 1981 season which Point won and meant that they had gone through the entire season without dropping a point. The Point team that season under John Crichton was in my eyes the best Point team I have seen and I feel privileged to have played a small part in it".

> "...The Point team that season under John Crichton was in my eyes the best Point team I have seen and I feel privileged to have played a small part in it."

John Crichton was the inspiration off the field; the player who drove them on the field was Robert MacKay. The players who played in that team speak fondly of the whole team but there is a consensus that Robert MacKay was the single most influential player. Robert really should not have been a Point player at all and there are shades of the past in the way that he was signed for Point." I signed for Point at the old Stornoway Airport in January 1979. I was met by John Crichton and Iain MacKenzie off the Inverness plane on a cold January day. I had already signed for the Aths but they would not listen to me so I signed to get rid of them. The rest is history!". It was a significant if unorthodox signing. Robert was not only an inspirational player he was also Player Manager with another stalwart Norman "Buck" MacAskill. Robert's assessment of the 1981 team is hugely revealing. Accepting that they were too strong for the other Lewis teams he says "but the team was only together for the one season".

Reading the reports of the matches played during the season it is clear that this was a team who did not just play good football but played for each other and were hugely ambitious in their aspirations. How else do you explain being 3-0 against Back at half time in the semi-final of the Acres Boys' Club and still winning 4-3? How many knew that on the morning of the Final Robert MacKay was taken to the doctor to have pain killing injections to allow him to play in the evening? They beat Ness 1-0 in the Final to win their first Cup. Another great team effort saw them beating Ness once again to win the Jock Stein Cup by 3-2. They beat Athletic 4-0 to win the Lewis Cup but they failed to win the Eilean an Fhraoich Cup.

Many supporters would say that they were the best team ever to represent Point but there would be just as many who could argue as strong a case for the team of the 1970s or that of the 1990s. These were also exceptional teams and showed a consistency over a period of time in the League that the team of 1981 did not do. In many ways the teams of the 1970s and 1990s could be compared to the United team of the late 1950s, the Athletic team of the 1960s and the Ness team of the 1980s and early 1990s. They maintained success over a longer period of time. My own view is that the 1981 team should be more properly compared to the brilliant School team of the mid 1950s. For a wonderful brief spell the 1981 Point team glittered like a star in the galaxy. They were a very fine team.

Chapter 7
Wider Horizons

Triumph in the
Highland Amateur Cup

In 1984 Ness Football Club decided to enter the Highland Amateur Cup. This was the beginning of a development in Lewis football which was to transform the game in the Island. The year 1984, therefore, becomes as important in the history of Lewis football as 1933, when the Eilean an Fhraoich Cup was introduced, and 1937, when the Lewis League was started. It heralded an expansion of horizons both geographical and sporting and offered Island footballers the opportunity to test their skills against different opponents.

As a football team Ness had been consistently successful and both their success and their ambitions coincided with Stornoway Football Association's recent membership of the Scottish Amateur Football Association. This gave Lewis clubs access to District and National competitions. Ness saw the opportunity and "the appointment of an ambitious new manager in John MacIver, backed by a progressive committee under the chairmanship of Calum Iain MacLeod, made the time ripe for Ness to put their aspirations to the test". (25).

In hindsight there is an inevitability about the move but at the time it was a revolutionary step which provided all Lewis Football Clubs with the opportunity to raise their aspirations and their ambitions. The Highland Amateur Cup is the most prestigious competition for teams from the north of Scotland and had been inaugurated in 1978. It would be good to say that teams from the Islands were welcomed with open arms. Because of travelling difficulties they were not. To an extent that is still the situation and the Minch is wrongly perceived to be a hurdle for teams from the mainland. Despite that it has undoubtedly changed perspectives in Lewis. Ness won the Cup at their very first attempt when they beat Bishopmill Villa from Elgin 4-1 in the Final. By the mid 1990s they had won the Highland Amateur Cup four times and had arguably developed into the most successful amateur team in the north of Scotland at that time. Their success and ambition were to

Lewis Cup Winners, 1991

Back row – G Morrison, K MacLeod, D Hanlon, K MacDonald, A MacLeod, A Wright, D MacDonald, G Smith, A MacKay, A Murray

Front row – D Nicolson, I Finlayson, P O' Donnell, R MacLeod, J I Murray, N MacDonald

open a door for Lewis clubs and set a new standard for all of them.

Point was one of the teams that accepted the new challenge. It was not to be easy although there was a certain sweetness to the fact that they met and won against Ness a few days after Ness had won the Highland Amateur Cup. This is how Ivor Frater puts it "We played against Ness at Garrabost the week after they had won the Highland Amateur Cup and a win would put them in a commanding position in the league. There was a large crowd with cars all the way to Claypark and up into Knock and several buses of Niseachs. There was a crowd right round the pitch that evening and it was a cracking atmosphere. We beat them 4-0 and played a game where everyone played well and everything we did worked. I felt twenty feet tall at the end of that game!"

But the 1980s were less successful years. The marvellously unique League win of 1981 was followed by twelve fallow years before the League was won again in 1993. There were, however, compensations. The Point team of the mid 1980s were to equal Back's record of winning the Eilean an Fhraoich Cup for three consecutive years – 1983, '84, and '85. Their win in 1983 looked pretty impossible after the first leg of their first round tie against Ness. They lost that leg 5-0. It must have been a miserable game in which to play your first game for Point. That is what happened to Ivor Frater. "I made my debut in the Eilean an Fhraoich up in Ness in 1983 in an emergency. I was taken away from sheep shearing that afternoon to drive up to Ness as due to work reasons the seniors were short of defenders. It was a baptism of fire". It certainly was.

In the second leg, however, they were to produce the greatest ever comeback in the history of the competition. At Knock in the second leg they won 9-0 to win 9-5 on aggregate. Ian Macaulay remembers it well. "In the return game at Knock we were 2-0 up at half time. John Crichton was going "hyper"

in the dressing room telling us we were going to win the game. Not only did we win but we missed a penalty!". As one supporter, John MacIver put it "The goals were going in like hailstones". The official Ness history calls that match "a night to be forgotten". "When the final whistle sounded", it relates, "there was a stunned silence amongst the Ness supporters as the reality of what they had witnessed began to dawn on them". (26).

Point went on to win the cup. That was an auspicious win because it was the year that saw the Golden Jubilee of the Eilean an Fhraoich Cup. They beat Back 3-2 in the Final with goals from Alexander MacKay (2) and Norman John MacDonald. It was Norman John who scored the only goal in the Final against Back in the following year when both he and Willie "Frogie" MacDonald showed that veterans still had their uses. Perhaps the most interesting game in that successful cup run in 1984 was the win against Harris whom they beat 11-0. That is the second highest score in the competition's history. (24). (cf MacLeod op cit p 22.). Their third successive win came against Harris whom they beat 5-1 in the Final. The goals were scored by Iain "Walrus" Morrison (3), Robert MacKay and Ivor Finlayson.

Despite the lack of League success, however, work was progressing quietly that would result in yet another marvellous Point team emerging to take their place among the greats. The late 1980s and early 1990s was a transitional stage for the club. A crop of young players came to the fore including Angus "Stoodie" MacKay, Donald "Tuf" MacDonald, George MacAskill, Ross MacLeod, Norrie "Minster" MacDonald, George Smith, Ivor Finlayson and later on Willie Macaulay. The goalkeeper was Alex Wright who was to become almost a legendary figure in the history of the club, still plying his trade as a goalkeeper in his 40s. By 1992 a team that could challenge for honours was coming together. In that season they almost won the League at a time when the great Ness team was still

ABC Cup Winners, 1992

Back row – K MacLeod, I Butterworth, A MacIver, P O' Donnell, A Wright, D MacDonald, A MacKay, K MacDonald, D Nicolson

Front row – J I Murray, R MacLeod, G Smith, I Finlayson, G MacAskill, D Hanlon

Eilean an Fhraoich Cup Winners, 1992

Back row – I Butterworth, K MacDonald, G Morrison, C Johnston, D Hanlon, A MacLeod, A MacKay, B Flower, G MacAskill, A MacKenzie, C MacLeod, I MacAulay, A Daniel

Front row – A MacIver, R MacLeod, N MacDonald, D MacDonald, P MacDonald, D Nicolson, R MacKay

Lewis Cup Winners, 1994

Back row – C MacLeod, K MacLeod, A Wright, G MacAskill, G Smith, D MacDonald, L MacLeod, A MacKay, D Hanlon

Front row – R Emerson, I Butterworth, R MacLeod, B Kennedy, I Finlayson

dominating Lewis football. One year later they became the first Point team since 1981 to win the League.

Nevertheless, the winning of the Highland Amateur Cup was the pinnacle of their success and the greatest achievement of any Point team over the 80 years of its history. It did not, however, happen overnight. There was a process of transition and development. As far as people like Angus "Stoodie" is concerned the arrival of Davie Hanlon as Player/Manager was the turning point as were his signings of George MacAskill and George Smith from Athletic and United respectively. There is an acceptance that Davie Hanlon was a sound tactician. "Charlton", for example valued his tactical awareness very highly. "Davie Hanlon was a student of the game. A fine player, I played with him at Tolsta and Point. He also managed Point during a successful period. In the amateur game the giving of advice is plentiful but the taking of it is rare. But he gave me some advice which I took on board. The advice was "play the way you're facing" – basically pass and move. Simple and effective".

"Camaraderie – the one word I associate during my time with Point – we had in abundance. The majority of us were all great friends and I think we brought that on to the park, as we'd fight tooth and nail for each other."

There were other reasons why this squad were so successful. Ross MacLeod puts it like this "Camaraderie – the one word I associate during my time with Point – we had in abundance. The majority of us were all great friends and I think we brought that on to the park, as we'd fight tooth and nail for each other." Just as significantly, he continues "we also had (and have) a

great respect for Malcolm Flower, our Chairman, and the rest of the committee (and past committees) who work so hard behind the scenes". It seems to be that this was one of these special moments when the whole club community was working as one. Whatever the reasons, the winning of the Cup in August, 1994 at Victoria Park in Dingwall was a wonderful achievement.

After a bye in the first round there was a narrow 3-2 away win against Stornoway United at Goathill in the second round with goals coming from Richard Emerson, George Smith and Davie Hanlon. Incredibly these two goals lost to United were the only goals conceded in the cup winning run. Another away tie saw them travel to Brora to take on the Orkney team, Kirkwall Accies, whom they easily beat 6-0. The goals were scored by Ivor Finlayson (4) and George Smith (2). A home tie followed against North Uist whom they beat 2-0 with Ivor and Donald "Tuf" MacDonald scoring. Then there were impressive wins in the quarter and semi finals over Pentland United and Alness. The game against Pentland United at Contin was an important one given that Pentland were the holders of the Cup and there is general agreement that this was probably Point's best performance in the cup. The game itself ended in a 0-0 draw but Point won 4-3 on penalties. Ross MacLeod, one of the players, is clear that "though this game went to penalties, it is regarded as the best game that Point played during the run. We totally dominated the game against a strong team who were favourites to beat us. We hit the woodwork on no less than four occasions and came up against an inspired goalkeeper".

The semi final performance against another of the favourites, Alness, at Grant Street, home of Inverness Clach, was a clinical performance. From early on in the game the result was never in doubt and the Gazette of August 18th saw the strength of the team emanating from the back. Angus "Stoodie" MacKay and George MacAskill, it commented, formed "the best central defensive partnership in north amateur football". Angus

"Stoodie" himself saw that the 3-0 win depended greatly on "our winger Richard Emerson taking advantage of the large pitch to put in a scintillating display". He scored two of the goals with Ivor Finlayson also scoring yet again. Going into the Final, Point, having beaten the two strongest teams in the tournament, were regarded as the favourites against Cromarty to take the Cup to Lewis for the fourth time.

> "The emotion before the start of the final was immense, with the bagpipes playing, our hearts pumping, it was hard to catch a breath – this team, after all, could go down in Point history!"

The Final itself was a heroic affair. Point had been weakened before the game started by the withdrawal through injury of Lewis "Sketch" MacLeod and Norrie "Minster" MacDonald. This meant that it was going to be difficult to control the midfield; so it turned out. The players themselves were a little apprehensive before the game. Angus "Stoodie" describes the dressing room as "nervous". They were quite well aware that this was not just a special game, they knew it was the most important game in the club's history. The team itself had travelled over to Dingwall on the Friday night and had stayed at the National Hotel in order to give them the best preparation for Saturday's final. Hundreds of the Point supporters who had travelled on the early morning ferry then gathered noisily at the hotel to remind them, as if they needed to be reminded, that this was no ordinary game. Ross MacLeod describes it like this "The emotion before the start of the final was immense, with the bagpipes playing, our hearts pumping, it was hard to catch a breath – this team, after all, could go down in Point history!".

The game itself went a long way to proving that the Gazette was correct in analysing where the strength of the team really did lie. Its report of the Final was headlined "Fine Defence wins Cup for Rudhachs" and it went on to define the Point defence as the Thin Red Line. The accepted hero of the hour was Alex Wright, the goalkeeper, who "broke Cromarty hearts with a string of saves, especially in the second half". Reflecting on the game almost a decade later Angus "Stoodie" is clear that the failure to score an early goal was significant. "Despite being the dominant team in the early stages we failed to score a goal and our play became a bit anxious in a scrappy game". Immediately after the game the Player/Manager David Hanlon conceded to the Gazette reporter that it had probably been their poorest performance in the Cup.

Yet they won. That consistent goal scorer, Ivor Finlayson, scored the goal that was to take the Highland Amateur Cup to Point. This is how the Gazette describes it. "Then came the moment of glory as a MacDonald free-kick found Ivor Finlayson in space and although his first effort was blocked he stroked home from eight yards to put Point ahead in 78 minutes". From then on the game became a rearguard action with Alex Wright making a number of key saves to seal a famous victory. But each and every one of the players deserve to be commended for sticking to their task and for ensuring that the Thin Red Line was not breached in the last hectic minutes. It was also apposite that the Gazette saw fit to congratulate all the others who had played their part. "Substitutes Iain "Fairy" Macaulay and Calum "Curly" MacLeod were not used, but in a campaign that started in May, they and others used to win the competition, were equal heroes to the faithful, and the committee that helped them to get there were not forgotten either as congratulations were being dished out". The match was over; the game was won; the Highland Amateur Cup was coming to Point for the first time; there was an overwhelming feeling of both relief and pride. It had been a magical day.

Highland Amateur Cup Winners, 1994

Back row – N MacDonald, D MacDonald, C MacLeod, G MacAskill, A Wright, D Hanlon, A MacKay, K MacLeod, A MacLeod

Front row – I MacAulay, R Emerson, G Smith, I Finlayson, I Butterworth, R MacLeod, B Kennedy

The magic continued after the game. The news that the "Suilven", the ferry from Ullapool to Stornoway, had mechanical problems and would be three hours late went down well with all except one supporter who had celebrated just a little too much. Let Angus "Stoodie" take up the story. "When we arrived in Ullapool at 7.30 pm we all got off the bus to go to the Seaforth Hotel except the said supporter whom we left sleeping on the bus. When he awoke on his own he looked at his watch, saw that there was no ferry and immediately panicked thinking he was stuck in Ullapool for the night. He stumbled to the phonebox to call his wife to tell her the news that he had missed the ferry but was told to sober up as the ferry had only just left Stornoway!". The ferry did make it back to Stornoway that night and it must have been an eventful journey. Ian "Fairy" Macaulay understates it when he refers to it as "oidhche mhor air a ferry". It most certainly was and despite the lateness of the hour supporters had gathered at the pier to welcome the team back to Lewis.

"oidhche mhor air a ferry"

It had been an eventful day and the memories still remain sweet. Ivor Finlayson remembers scoring the only goal in the Final as the most outstanding memory of his career. The view of the supporters is well represented by two of the spectators at the game who make exactly the same comment. Both Iain MacSween and Calum Alasdair Campbell remember the game as their outstanding memory of supporting the team and mention in particular the display of Alex Wright in goals. Some would argue that Point have had teams since 1994 who probably should have won the Highland Amateur Cup again. But none has and the team of 1994 has a special place in the hearts of all Point supporters.

It is, I think, important to record who played in that eventful Final. They will always carry the distinction of being the first team to take the Highland Amateur Cup to Point. They wrote their own significant chapter in the history of the team. The players were Alex Wright; Ross MacLeod; Iain Butterworth; George MacAskill; Angus MacKay; Donald C MacDonald; George Smith; Bobby Kennedy; David J Hanlon; Ivor Finlayson and Richard A Emerson. The substitutes were Calum MacLeod and Iain M Macaulay.

Under the guidance of manager Davie Hanlon, and latterly Angus "Stoodie" MacKay, Norman "Squiggles" MacKenzie and Donald "Tuf" MacDonald the team went on to win the League in 1993, 1996, 1997, 1998, 2002 and 2004, the Eilean an Fhraoich Cup four times, the Coop Cup four times, the Jock Stein Cup four times and the Acres Cup on four occasions. It is extremely important to itemise these successes in detail because there is a tendency to identify the team of this particular era solely with the triumph of winning the Highland Amateur Cup in 1994. That, of course, was the team's most momentous achievement and the one that brought them most public acclaim but it must not overshadow the rest of their successes. In any language this was one of the greatest teams that have represented Point and they also stand beside the other great Lewis teams in terms of what they achieved and also in terms of their consistency over many seasons. In the context of the history of the club they vie with the team of the 1970s as the most consistently successful Point team of all time.

League Champions, 1998

Back row – W MacAulay, N MacDonald, D Hanlon, A MacKay, D Libby, G Craigie, D MacDonald, G Miller, D Murray, I MacKenzie

Front row – A Wright, I A Afrin, R MacLeod, I Butterworth, G MacAskill, C MacLeod, G Smith, I Finlayson

Point Seniors and Juniors, 1998

Back row – D MacKenzie, K McCarvel, C MacKay, A Inglis, A Joyce, J A Munro, I Finlayson, D Hanlon, A MacKay, R MacLeod, I A Afrin, D Libby,
I MacKenzie, G Miller, D MacDonald, G Smith, D Murray, N MacDonald

Front row – A Hadidi, M MacIver, S Campbell, N MacSween, C MacKenzie

Chapter 8
The Modern Era

The Challenges

In its first edition of the year 2000 the Stornoway Gazette carried the headline "Welcome to the new Millennium" and reported that the "winter weather on the last day of the century failed to dampen the spirits of the many who turned out to watch the Millennium firework display organised by the Round Table". Inside the paper there was a wonderful article on William MacKenzie, Bard Cnoc Cusbaig from Shader, and an equally inspirational piece on the renowned Gaelic singer, Joan MacKenzie (Seonag Smidge) from Garrabost. Her CD of Gaelic songs was regarded as the best recording of the last year of the century. All Rubhachs would have read that with pleasure.

On the football front there was an interesting article in the Gazette of the 10th February by Malcolm MacDonald, the chief football reporter, bemoaning the fact that top Scottish football clubs are not interested in fostering the game in the islands. "Let us hope", he said. "that with a new century attitudes will have changed and that football fans will have the opportunity to watch top class footballers at first hand". Although Dundee United visited the Island later that year it is clear that there still exists a peripheral area in Scottish football that is not supported by the professional game. That has always been the case and it is to be hoped that the situation will improve as travelling becomes easier and football administrators become more aware of their responsibilities to footballers throughout Scotland.

This is important because there are wider issues inherent in today's football world which will encroach on football in the Islands. To some extent modern football is now influenced by the power of television. Will such coverage inhibit people from going to watch a level of football which is by definition of a different quality? It might. How can football administrators in Scotland help football in the peripheral areas of the country? One of the present Point team, Donald Robert MacIver, suggested to me that the time has come to finance feeder

Cup Display, 2002 – League, Acres Boys Club, Eilean an Fhraoich and Co-op Cup Winners

Back row – D Murray, A Joyce, G Dunn, G Smith, A Wright, A MacKay, I MacKenzie, D MacDonald, D Libby, A MacKay

Front row – W MacAulay, D MacIver, I MacIver, C Kerr, C MacKay, R MacLeod, C Robertson

League & Jock Stein Cup Winners, 2004

Back row – G Kennedy, D Murray, A MacKay, G Smith, W MacAulay, I A Afrin, S Lennie, S Liddle, S MacDonald, I MacKenzie, A Wright

Front row – M MacIver, A Joyce, C MacKay, I MacIver, D MacIver, C Adams, A MacKay,

Co-op Cup & Eilean an Fhraoich Cup Winners, 2005
Back row – S Lennie, S MacDonald, D MacLean, D MacLeod, I MacKenzie, S Liddle, I A Afrin, A MacIver, S MacPherson, K MacLeod, N MacKay, M MacLeod, C MacKay, A MacKay
Front row – W MacAulay, G Smith, C MacKay, D Black, M MacIver, I MacIver

clubs in cities like Glasgow for Island teams. There are now so many young lads, he argues, leaving the island but with easy travelling opportunities to play in the island that there is a case to be made for radical thinking. In many ways it would be a development of the philosophy that created the Eilean an Fhraoich Cup, but this time it would be the island itself influencing the thinking in Glasgow. There should not exist in Scotland a class of enthusiastic amateur footballers, trapped by their geography, who are effectively "children of the periphery".

In terms of Lewis football the Point team have never been on the periphery, yet it would be true to say that the years following the advent of the new Millennium have not been their most consistent. As the old century ended they were pipped at the post for the League title in the 1999 season by Ness and in a close run for the League in the following season they were beaten into third place by Back and Harris. In many ways that first season of the Millennium was a portent of things to come as the 21st century unfolded. They were beaten for the League by Back, they lost 3-1 to Harris in the Final of the Lewis Cup and were "swept aside" by Back in the Eilean an Fhraoich Cup Final to the tune of 6-0. Yet they won the Acres Cup when they beat Ness 4-1 and their true place in Lewis football was captured by the Gazette when it described the trophy being handed over Donald "Tuf" MacDonald, the Point captain, "to show that Point are still giants in island football".

Within two years they were showing that they were indeed a substantial force in Lewis football. In 2004 they won the Jock Stein Cup against Ness after penalties. Managed by Angus "Stoodie" MacKay they also took the League title. "It was", he said, "a magnificent achievement over the season despite a strong challenge from Back and Lochs". Both these rivals had strong teams during these years. Back, for example, won the Highland Amateur Cup that year – the seventh Island win since Ness first entered in 1984. Lochs beat Point 2-1 in the

final of the Eilean an Fhraoich Cup and went on to win the Highland Amateur Cup the following season when they beat Avoch 3-1. This was the third year in a row that Lewis teams had triumphed in the competition. They also won the League but in the Co-op Cup Final Point beat them in a game that went to penalties and is remembered for the "sensational form" of the Point goalkeeper, David Black. In the same season, 2005, Point also won the Eilean an Fhraoich Cup when they beat Back in the Final by 2-0. The goals were scored by the brothers from Bayble, Calum "Cally" MacKay and Ali "Bubble" MacKay. A young player like Donald Robert MacIver could say that by 2005 he had won two League medals in 2002 and 2004, an Eilean an Fhraoich Cup medal, a Lewis Cup medal and a Jock Stein Cup medal. "I got them all", he says, "except the Amateur Cup".

That particular medal certainly did elude him and his colleagues as they tried to emulate the feat of the 1994 team. In 2007 Point reached yet again the final of the Highland Amateur Cup. In the first round, away from home, they beat Uist United 4-0 with the goals coming from Robert MacLeod, Donald MacDonald (2) and Daniel Keenan. In the second round they sqeezed past their old rivals Back by a single goal scored by Innes "Fushie" MacIver. A hat trick from Cally MacKay against Wick Rovers in a match played at Fortrose saw them into the Quarter Final where they beat Dingwall Thistle 3-0 with the goals coming from the MacKay brothers and Steven Liddle. The game against John O'Groats in the semi final was a bruising encounter played at Culbokie. Alex Wright, that astonishing veteran, was the hero saving a 93rd minute penalty to send the game to extra time. The only goal of the game was then scored by Iain Andrew Afrin. For the second time a Point team had reached the final of the Highland Amateur Cup. It was a creditable achievement that was to end disappointingly in the final when they lost 5-0 to Avoch. It was a poor display by the Reds at a damp and dreary Grant

Point FC, St. Etienne, France in 1998 (World Cup)

Back row – A. MacMillan (piper), C I MacMillan, D MacSween, A MacKay, D MacDonald, R MacLeod, D MacDonald, M J Graham, C MacLeod, G Smith, I MacKenzie, I A Afrin, C MacKenzie, W MacAulay, C MacKinnon, C Frater

"Point beat St Etienne 3-2 in the final, the first Scottish team ever to return from the World Cup with a trophy and medals"

Street Park in Inverness. They were outplayed and outclassed by a slick Avoch team which has traditionally been one of the strongest amateur teams in the north of Scotland.

That particular final, despite the heavy defeat, was nevertheless the highlight of a club that was so obviously developing a new young team at this time. The players who made up the squad for that Final were Alex Wright, David "Psycho" MacIver, Angus "Stoodie" MacKay, Stuart Macpherson, Iain "Macca" MacKenzie, Donald "Rab" MacIver, Andrew Joyce, Iain Andrew "Afo" Afrin, Steven Liddle, Daniel Keenan, Calum "Cally" MacKay, Willie Macaulay, Scott "Scotty Bomb" Campbell, Andrew "Joycie" Joyce, Stuart MacLeod and Neil "Kai" MacKay. Their manager was Donald "Tuf" MacDonald who had distinguished himself so often as a player. He did, of course, have a pedigree. His family had given so much service to the football club over the years. His uncle Willie "Frogie" was a legendary goalkeeper and his father, Kenny Dan, was a loyal and determined Chairman of the club.

Interestingly, as Point were going through this transitional phase, so were their traditional rivals, Back. It is ironic that in the very year, 2009, that the rivalry between Point and Back was commemorated in an exhibition of memorabilia at Hampden both their fortunes were at a low ebb. Point had actually won the Jock Stein Cup in 2008 but that has been the last trophy won by the Club. In a preview of the 2009 season the Gazette could comment on 9 April that "when either one of the Broadbay two falls from the heights to which they are accustomed they fall hard". Point, who had been Champions in 2004 finished 7th in 2008 and 6th in 2009. In an interview with the Gazette on 8 April 2010 their veteran Goalkeeper, Alex Wright, said quite rightly "I think getting to a cup final would be tremendous progress for us as we are a young side going through a transitional phase". And this realistic view of the world will carry the club to further triumphs although it will always be tied to a belief in the club and what it stands for.

"Never fear" said the Club Chairman, Malcolm Flower, "the good times will come back".

That, of course, will happen. Football success, like any other, will ebb and flow. Nevertheless, there are significant challenges ahead. There was alarm expressed for example, in the Gazette of March 2, 2000 that the Registrar General for Scotland was projecting that the population of the Western Isles would drop from 27,940 to 23,980 by 2016. That has indeed happened earlier than was predicted and with these figures come a severe challenge to the future health of a team game like football in the Islands. In a world of population decline and other sporting attractions there is a very real challenge to football in the Islands in the next few years of the 21st century. Already it is clear that individual sports like Athletics are becoming more popular and more successful than ever before in the Western Isles and a new phenomenon like the Island Games is bound to be attractive in an era when travel has become easier. Added to that is the fact that the North Sea Oil industry takes away young men from the Island in the same way as the Merchant Navy did in the 1950s. That is the price that Islands will always pay. Many of their young will inevitably leave.

The lack of a substantial population base carries with it a few worries. There has always been in Lewis football the occasional movement of players from one club to another but for the most part most players have played for their own Districts or their own local teams. The original rules of the Eilean an Fhraoich Cup were devised to encourage this kind of territorial loyalty. It would be foolish to deny that this state of affairs can continue if the population continues to decline and there is now evidence to suggest that many players do not come from their own Districts. Does that imply a lack of commitment to the jersey? Not necessarily, but it could signal a significant change in the whole ethos of Lewis football. After all, football in the island was founded on the concept of village and District teams. Teams in the town of Stornoway were different but they

Point Team, 2009

Back row – A Murray, S MacLeod, A MacKay, I MacKenzie, I Gillies, Duncan MacKenzie (Sponsor), A Wright, S MacPherson, J MacDonald, D Hunter

Front row – C MacKay, D R MacIver, A Murray, D MacKenzie, K Stewart, C Ross, I Lamont, D MacLean

Ionad Stoodie

have always had a larger catchment area; and no one can deny the loyalty and commitment to the town shown over the years by teams like Athletic and United.

If the original concept is to be maintained then much weight will need to be placed on how well each team develops its own youth. As a football club Point has always been aware of the importance of rearing its own young. When I interviewed Iain "Sheordie" MacKenzie from Bayble he went to great lengths to ensure that I was aware of the thread that runs through the history of the Club in terms of nurturing young talent. From the very beginnings of village football in the early 1930s this development can be seen. In the 1950s, for example, Bayble were hugely successful in competitions like the Junior League (founded in 1945 just after the war), the Kemnay Cup and the Roma Cup.

Over the years many adults have given much of their time, expertise and knowledge to ensure that a stream of young players are fed through to the senior team. Most of them are former players. Some like Donald John Murray from Shader could say that "I did not play an awful lot of games but I was heavily involved in running Point Junior teams from 1978 through to 1987 and then from 1999 through to the present time". Others like Alex Dan Campbell did play regularly over many years and managed the Point Junior team that won the treble of the League, the Ladywell and Cuach a' Phaipear Bhig competitions in 1985. Others pay tribute to people like "Buck" MacAskill who, insists Donald Duncan MacIver, "was great with youngsters". But the commitment remains and the present management team are heavily involved in supporting and developing the youth of the District.

That is the football challenge. There is another one for the Club and that is to continue its close involvement with the community itself. As the 20th century came to an end it was clear that this tie was as strong as ever. In 1998 the football team was an integral part of a cultural exchange visit to St Etienne in France organised by Pròiseact nan Ealan, the Gaelic Arts Agency. This involved fifty Rubhachs spending a week in the city as part of a Scottish/French/Moroccan exchange. They were cultural ambassadors at the World Cup Finals which were being held in France that summer. The fact that Point won the football tournament that was part of the exchange prompted the official report of the trip to comment "Point beat St Etienne 3-2 in the final, the first Scottish team ever to return from the World Cup with a trophy and medals". (27). It was, of course, much more than a visit to another European country. It reinforced the commitment of a football team to its own community; and it illustrated at the same time how much the community valued its football team. In this situation football becomes part of a much bigger picture. The Gazette of 10 June, 1998 could report that "the Jock Stein Cup Final due to be played on 19 June has become a victim of the World Cup and will now be rearranged at a later date. Finalists Point are in France for ten days with their community as part of the footballing bonanza over the period and the game will now be rescheduled as agreed by the Lewis and Harris football Association before the season". As it happened Point went on to win the Cup beating Athletic in the final.

How appropriate, then, to leave eighty years of history with that particular thought - success on the field running parallel to success within its own community. That has been the thread running through the history of this proud club. In terms of the amount of trophies won it has become the most successful football club in the history of Lewis football. That has been its success on the field; off the field it has been just as successful. It has brought a sense of pride to the whole Point community and it has shown itself to be the champion of the District at the very times when the community needed that leadership. It has been a proud history.

Chapter 9
Conclusion

Voices from the Club

Football is a passionate affair. Supporting any club becomes a way of life and supporters become the life blood of any club. When researching this book I discovered that all who have been associated with the Club over the years are, without apology, aware of a strong and sometimes raw sense of identity, loyalty and emotional tie to the football Club and to the District of Point itself.

This is better illustrated in the commitment of Murdo MacLeod (Biodan Narrow) from Broker than in any one else. A history of Point Football Club would not be complete without a special mention of the Biodan. He was 7 years old when he saw Point play for the first time in 1939 and thus began a love affair which has lasted a lifetime. He played first for Point in 1948 when he was 16 and has been involved in the life of the team ever since. He was a member of the great team that won the League in 1951, 52, 54 and 1956. He has been involved with the Club in every conceivable way and was an integral part of the process that brought Point its own football pitch to Knock in the 1970s. Much of his life has been devoted to the football club and also to the Point community at large. He had the satisfaction of seeing his son, Ross, become a regular member of the of the hugely successful team of the 1990s. He talks with great pride of the fact that he was presented with a plaque to commemorate 50 years of association with the club. The truth of the matter is that his association has lasted much longer than that. It would be true to say that it has lasted a lifetime.

And there have been others. Point has had its share of fervent supporters but none more so than Murdo MacMillan from Shader who was perhaps the most faithful supporter of them all. Murdo was a strong, hard-working man, at one time having a horse, cart and plough with which he worked the village crofts. He then became an integral part of his brother Iain's burgeoning grocery business and was a fixture in the shop at the road end in Shader. But those commitments were cast aside if Point were playing. The "Assistant Manager" never missed a game and appeared, a James Cagney lookalike, in all the pictures of victorious teams. When the Hampden Museum of Football mounted an exhibition of football rivalries in which Point and Back featured in 2009 it was fitting that a photograph of Murdo, proudly holding the Eilean an Fhraoich Cup and with the Point scarf draped round his neck, should appear prominently amongst the exhibits. Murdo was the proudest ex-officio member that any team has ever had. He deserves his own personal paragraph in any history of Point Football Club.

At the time of writing this book the oldest surviving player was Angus Munro ("Unna") from Knock. I interviewed him at his home in the summer of 2012 when he spoke in clear and enthusiastic terms about the post war team in which he played following his demob in 1945. It was impossible not to notice that sitting proudly in his front room was a framed photograph of the Point team of 1947. In the course of the interview he mentioned more than once that "The team counted a lot then in Point".

But his was not just a parochial view of football. Here was a man who knew his football. He talked knowledgeably about tactics of his days and he talked glowingly of the professional players who had impressed him. Eusebio of Benfica and Portugal was his favourite player but "Bobby Charlton was the finest player I've ever seen". That same depth of knowledge about football emerged quite clearly from the responses I had from former players to my questionnaire. They were well aware of the tactics that were adopted in their own eras from the well defined rigidity of the 1930s to the fluidity and flexibility of the present day. They knew their football. What was even more striking was their appreciation of the football talents that were so apparent in other Lewis football teams. Each and every one of them was generous in naming the players from other teams who had impressed them. There was a healthy respect for the individual talents that make football the beautiful game.

Malcolm Flower, Chairman of Point FC Committee with Murdo MacLeod (Biodan Narrow) of Broker who was honoured for 50 years service to the club in 2001

Nevertheless, playing for Point was obviously a major part of their lives and the sense of loyalty to the club is so apparent. The present Secretary of the Club, Iain MacSween from Shader, who was not a player himself, put it this way "It is the most fundamental of loyalties which is sustained through everyday social interaction, not something which is expressed or exaggerated through mass media. It is different to supporting a professional or national team, it is much more about your identity". Another non-player but faithful follower, Callum Alasdair Campbell from Aird, expressed the same sense of identity when he said "Regardless of where you are living in later life you should always support the place of your birth and where you grew up".

Similar feelings came through other responses I received from the questionnaire. That great servant of the Club, John Crichton, probably spoke for many former players when he wrote "I don't think I can find words to explain what it meant to pull that jersey over my head". George MacAskill (Senior), from Shader, described it as "a privilege and honour" to play for Point and another stalwart, Alex Dan Campbell from Aird, wrote to me to say that it was "great to wear the red jersey and to play with such great players who played for the jersey".

No one could fail but be moved by the sentiments that came from John Graham (Iain Pheatarain) from Flesherin. Those who have followed the Club over the years know just how much Iain Pheatarain gave to Point Football Club. He started playing for Point Juniors in 1954, he played for the Senior team from 1955 to 1969 and he managed the Club from 1970 to 1974. In response to the question "Who were the outstanding Point players in your era?" he answered "Every boy who wore the Point jersey" and when he was asked to explain what it meant to be involved with Point Football Club he said quite simply "It was my life".

What has also come through from many of the former players is a sense of family continuity. When I interviewed my brother, Donald Duncan, it was immediately clear that he was immensely proud of the fact that two of his own sons, Matthew and Donald Robert, had played for the Club and had carried on a family tradition. Yet another former player from Shader voiced exactly the same sentiments. Donald John Murray did not play many games for Point but he was a Committee member and has given much to the running of Point Junior teams from 1978 to the present. He was immensely proud every time he took to the pitch in a Point shirt but "I take even greater pride now in watching my own son Andrew play. He has been a regular for the last four seasons and he is everything in a footballer that I had hoped to be". How similar that was to the submission from Malcolm Flower, the club's Chairman, who was quite clear that one of his most important memories was "watching my young nephew Stuart Flower playing for Point and winning Player of the Year 2011 in his first full season".

That same sense of pride was evident when I was asked by the Biodan to view the medals won by his son, Ross, when playing for Point. He took me upstairs in his home in Broker where the medals are carefully kept and savoured. Yet I did not see his own medals! He had won quite a few playing for the very fine 1950s team. His sense of pride lay in those won by Ross. But the feeling of family pride is reciprocated. Ross is "very proud of my dad's association with Point" and understands just how much his father gave of his time over the years to the club. He describes his mother as a "football widow". His father and mother married in 1962 and went on honeymoon to Blackpool. "Dad noticed Blackpool had a home game, gave mum enough money to buy a new coat and he went to the football himself". He does admit that it was "a beautiful green coat". It probably would have gone down better with his father had it been red!

The strong feeling of family was apparent in my interview with Ian "Fairy" Macaulay at his home in Sandwick. Ian, who played most of his football in the 1980s, is immersed in the history of the Club and has an enormously detailed knowledge of individual games and talks with authority about them. His commitment to the team is total. "I followed them as a supporter from 12, played for a very successful team – one of the best in Lewis football - and then managed them when they needed help." Yet he is still

Point U-18 Champions, 1986
Back row – A Steele, D MacKay, A MacDonald, I MacAulay, W Gillies, E MacDonald, K MacDonald
Front row – N Smith, A MacLeod, A MacKay, C MacKenzie, P MacPherson, C Nicolson, A D Campbell

the son of Pringle Macaulay from Shader who played for Point in the 1950s. When I asserted that his father was probably one of the most elegant and sophisticated players who had ever worn the red jersey he was quite overcome. He admitted that his father had been his football teacher in a pitch at the back of their house in Shader. It was clear that he took a great feeling of comfort from the fact that his father had seen him winning all his medals. The family legacy he had inherited had been, he admitted, the motivating force behind his own loyalty to the Club.

That feeling of family commitment to the Club came to the fore in the submission I received from Norrie Tomsh. Norrie was no mean player himself but he impressed upon me the achievements of his brother Kenny MacDonald who was signed by Dundee United in 1986. Point had an outstanding team at that time with three exceptionally talented youngsters – Alistair "Herc" MacLeod, Eric MacDonald and Kenny MacDonald. They were so good that a letter was written by the Point Secretary to every team in the Premier League offering them for trial at the expense of Point FC. Kenny was picked up by Jim Maclean at Dundee United. Unfortunately he arrived at Tannadice in a year which saw Dundee United reach the UEFA Cup Final with a team of internationalists. He played a few games for the reserve team but finished his playing career with Edinburgh Spartans. Nevertheless his achievements are exceptional and it must have given great satisfaction to the Secretary of the Club to have written that letter in November 1985. The Secretary just happened to be Kenny's father, Norman MacDonald (Tarmod Tomsh).

And there was another son – Iver who also played for Point. He wrote to me in exactly the same kind of terms. "My father, Tarmod Tomsh, and many of his friends played for Point in the 1950s so there was an expectation that we should at least aspire to play for Point. Many a time I turned up to watch a game with my boots in the back of the car just in case I got that call. Playing with my brother Norrie in the team seemed like normal progression, but now as I get older I realise it was a privilege that not many brothers get".

It is clear then that this is a Club which inspires loyalty from cradle to grave. Let me, therefore, leave the last word to Ivor Frater from Bayble who played in the 1980s and describes himself as "never the most elegant player in the world" but "I played for the jersey". This is what he wrote to explain to the world how it felt to play for the red jersey.

> "I am proud to be a Rubhach and on every occasion I played for Point I always put on my shirt last. I felt it was a privilege to be savoured."

"When I was a young boy in Bayble, television football was rare and generally on late, with the only exposure to the wide world being newspapers and radio commentaries. The only tangible football was local football and as I walked up the road there were the red shirts of Norman "Tarmod Snosh" MacDonald, Angus MacAskill and the green jersey of Buck MacAskill on the washing lines. I went on my bike to watch the team whenever I was allowed. After I made the team I used to go to the back of our house just to see the Point shirt I had worn fluttering on the line and to think how lucky I was. I am proud to be a Rubhach and on every occasion I played for Point I always put on my shirt last. I felt it was a privilege to be savoured".

Ivor may not have regarded himself as an elegant player but he writes elegantly and his eloquent words seem to me to encapsulate the history of Point Football Club. They evoke passion, commitment, loyalty to the team, a feeling and respect for the past and a tremendous pride in the District of Point. I hope that I have done justice to these feelings in this history of Point Football Club and I have no doubt that when the next history of the Club is written these feelings will still be as strong as they are now.

Point Team - Highland Amateur Cup, Round 1, 2nd May 2014 (Point 3 - Lochs 1)

Back row – W MacAulay (Assist Manager), S Flower, R Millar, C MacLean, A Wright, S Campbell, S Munro, S MacLeod, D Hunter, A MacKay (Manager)

Front row – S Kettings, A MacDonald, D R MacIver, A MacIver, K MacPhee, S Smith, S MacSween, A Khalil

Missing from this photo is – D MacLeod, D MacLennan, A Gillies, A MacMillan, J Guilmartin

Murdo MacMillan 'Assistant Manager', Shader

Willic John 'Teddy' Campbell

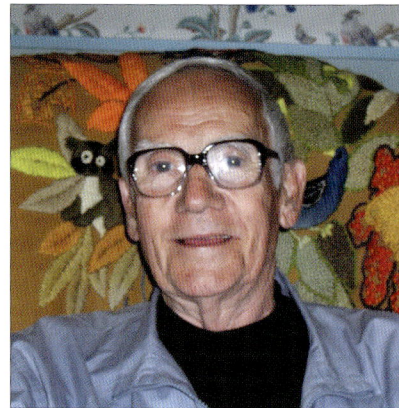

Alasdair MacDonald

Donald MacDonald (Freush), John MacKenzie (Seonaidh Fhoinnlaidh)

Donnie 'Dodo' Wilson

Cup display, 2004 – League Cup, Eilean an Fhraoich Cup, Acres Boys Club Cup and Co-op Cup winners
Malcolm Flower, Willie John 'Teddy', Alasdair Sheonaidh MacDonald, Murdo 'Biodan', Kenny D MacDonald, Andy Walsh, Angus 'Fushie' MacIver

Ionad Stoodie Opening, July 2007
L to R – Matt Bruce, Murdo 'Biodan' MacLeod,
Alastair MacDonald, Ronnie MacKinnon,
John Greig, Malcolm Flower

POINT FC RECORD OF ACHIEVEMENT

FORMED – 1934   **COLOURS** – Red & White
GROUND – Knock   **YEARS IN LEAGUE** – 1937-58, 1960 to date

71 Titles & Cups won in their 80 year history

LEAGUE CHAMPIONS

Winners (17): 1951, 1952, 1954, 1956, 1967, 1970, 1971, 1973, 1974, 1977, 1981, 1993, 1996, 1997, 1998, 2002, 2004
Runners-Up (13): 1937, 1946, 1947, 1961, 1964, 1968, 1975, 1980, 1983, 1985, 1986, 1992, 1999

EILEAN AN FHRAOICH CUP

Winners (17): 1934, 1935, 1937, 1952, 1953, 1965, 1966, 1970, 1973, 1975, 1983, 1984, 1985, 1992, 1998, 2002, 2005
Runners-Up (11): 1938, 1947, 1949, 1960, 1964, 1969, 1972, 1974, 1989, 2000, 2004

JOCK STEIN CUP

Winners (8): 1981, 1984, 1985, 1986, 1993, 1996, 1998, 2004
Runners-Up (3): 1977,1983, 2003

LEWIS CUP

Winners (5): 1967, 1973, 1974, 1981, 1991, 1995
Runners-Up (9): 1969, 1980, 1990, 1996, 1997, 2000, 2002, 2003, 2006

ACRES BOYS' CLUB CUP

Winners (6): 1981, 1986, 1992, 1997, 1998, 2002
Runners-Up (7): 1984, 1993, 1996, 1999, 2000, 2003, 2004

HIGHLAND AMATEUR CUP

Winners (1): 1994

CO-OP CUP

Winners (4): 1998, 1999, 2002, 2005

STORNOWAY CUP

Winners (5): 1953, 1954, 1956, 1960, 1963

Runners-Up (1): 1952

D'OYLY CARTE CUP

Winners (2): 1946, 1951

LEWIS CHALLENGE CUP (BUCHANAN CUP)

Winners (3): 1935, 1936, 1938

Runners-Up (1): 1939

TORMOD MOR TANKARD

Winners (1): 1947

Runners-Up (2): 1956, 1957

SUMMER CUP

Winners (1): 1974

AUTUMN CUP

Runners-Up (1): 1978

The medals from top to bottom read as –

Clachnacudden F.C., J MacDonald, N of S Junior League, N of S Junior Cup 1949-50

Lewis Football Association League Winners 1952 Point F.C.

J.C. 1951

Point F.C. Lewis Football League Champions - Season 1955

John 'Hoddan' MacDonalds medals which were kindly donated to the club by his family

References

1. The Islands Book Trust: "Island Emigrants". The Islands Book Trust, 2009. P168.

2. F.G.Rea: "A School in South Uist". Birlinn, 1997. P143.

3. Calum Ferguson: "Lewis in the Passing". Birlinn, 2007. P299.

4. Ibid. P305.

5. Football in Ness, Acair, 2000. P7 - 8.

6. Carloway FC Website.

7. cf Angus Graham : "Eilean an Fhraoich Cup". Back in the Day, February, 2013. P22.

8. Calum Smith: "Around the Peat – Fire". Birlinn, 2001. P72.

9. Ibid. P117.

10. Carol Gow: "Mirror and Marble". Saltire, 1992. P11.

11. Back Football Club. 75th Anniversry, 1933-2008. P10.

12. D.J. MacLeod, Crossbost. North Lochs Newsletter.

13. Kenny MacLeod: "Eilean an Fhraoich Cup". Stornoway Gazette, 2003. P5.

14. Iain MacSween. 2009.

15. cf. Kenny MacLeod: "Eilean an Fhraoich Cup 1933-2003". Stornoway Gazette, 2003. P6.

16. cf MacLeod. P7.

17. cf Stornoway Historical Society Journal, July 2013.

18. A.Graham: op cit P22.

19. Rudhach, September, 2013.

20. "Sop as gach Seid", August 2010. P15.

21. cf Jack Rollin "Soccer at War 1939–45". Willow Books, 1985. P451.

22. Feu Charter by Stornoway Trustees in favour of Point Athletic Association, 1950.

23. Souvenir Programme. Point FC v Rangers FC U-19s, 16th July 2007.

24. Feu Disposition by the Stornoway Trust in favour of Trustees for Point Recreation Club. 1985.

25. "Football in Ness. Acair, 2000. P63.

26. Ibid. P61.

27. Pròiseact nan Ealan "A Cultural Visit to St Etienne, France. August, 1998. P20.

Appendix 1

Questionnaire

The following people responded to the questionnaire -

Alex Dan Campbell, Stornoway and Aird

Calum Alasdair Campbell, Aird

Iain Crichton, Knock

Ivor Finlayson, Flesherin

Malcolm Flower, Knock

Ivor Frater, Kilmarnock and Bayble

John Graham, Back and Flesherin

George MacAskill (Snr), Stornoway

George MacDonald, Bayble

Iver MacDonald, Edinburgh and Aird

Norrie MacDonald, Aird

Angus MacKay, Garrabost

Robert MacKay, Aignish

Murdo MacLeod, Broker

Ross MacLeod, Broker

Iain MacSween, Shader

Angus Murray, New Tolsta and Swordale

Donald John Murray, Shader

Interviews

The following people were formally interviewed for the book -

Ian MacAulay, Sandwick   11th July, 2012

Donald Duncan MacIver, Portnaguran   11th July, 2012

Donald Robert MacIver, Portnaguran   13th July, 2012

Iain MacKenzie, Stornoway and Bayble   4th January, 2013

Murdo MacLeod, Broker   11th July, 2012

Ross MacLeod, Broker   12th March, 2013

Angus Munro, Knock   2th July, 2012

Photographs

The following people sent me photographs -

Ivor Finlayson, Flesherin

George MacAskill (Snr), Stornoway

Norrie MacDonald, Aird

Mrs Alina MacLeod, Aird and Ness

Iain MacSween, Shader

Additional Information

I received additional information from the following people -

Ian MacAulay, Sandwick and Shader

Calum Iain MacDonald, Coll, Back

Norrie MacDonald, Aird

Rob MacLeod, Leurbost, Lochs

Ross MacLeod, Broker

Iain MacSween, Shader

Appendix 2

The Questionnaire

The History of Point Football Club

I am presently writing a history of Point Football Club to commemorate its 80th Anniversary in 2014. I have discovered that so many people want to contribute their thoughts that I simply cannot interview everyone. What I am doing, therefore, is to try to send this simple questionnaire to as many people as I can. It would be marvellous if you could find a few minutes to send me some thoughts. Some of the questions will not apply to you. I understand that but any information will be gratefully accepted. Every single response will be acknowledged in the book.

If you have relevant photographs that would be even better. They would all be returned once the book is ready for publication.

Thank you for your help.

When did you play for Point eg the 50s, 60s, 70s, etc?

If you were not a player how were you involved?

Who were the outstanding Point players in your era?

Who were the outstanding players for other teams in your era? Who were the outstanding teams in Lewis at that time?

Football tactics have changed dramatically in the 80 years since Point Football Club was set up? What tactics were employed in your era? What are your outstanding memories? This may include actual incidents rather than say Cup Finals or other notable games.

Can you explain what it meant to you to play for, or to be involved with, Point Football Club.

All responses should be sent to me at my home address at:

Matthew MacIver

21 Durham Road

Edinburgh EH15 1NY

or to my email address at -

matthew.maciver@myportnaguran.co.uk

Moran taing.

Appendix 3
The Highland Amateur Cup, 1994

I Know 'Cos I was there

'Twas on the 25th of August
The day it dawned quite fair
When the Rudhachs went across the Minch,
I know 'cos I was there.
To Dingwall Town we were bound
We got up with the lark
To follow our team, 'The Red Machine'
All the way to County's Park.

I'll never forget that famous day
When history was made
When the Rudhachs won the Highland Cup
I know 'cos I was there.
We've followed the team through thick and thin
In friendlies, leagues and cups
But that was the one that made our day
When we won the Highland Cup.

The play it raged from end to end
It was exciting stuff
Our goalkeeper, that famous day
Was a hero right enough.
The team that played us on that day
Came out with style and flair
But the Point defence broke all their hearts
I know 'cos I was there.

Then came their greatest moment
That I will never forget
Ivor came from nowhere and the ball was in the net.
We cried, we laughed, we sung, we danced,
A roar it filled the air
The day we won the Highland Cup
I know 'cos I was there.

Homeward bound from Ullapool
With laughter and with tears
Began the celebrations with whisky and with beer
I still think it was all a dream.
And to be absolutely fair,
When the Suilven berthed in town that night
I couldn't remember being there!

Willie John 'Teddy' Campbell

Appendix 4

Another poem from one of the "Grumblies"

Independence for Point

You can talk about your Holyrood
The Labour the Lib-Dems or even Tory blue
But give to me the party
Who will make my dream come true
By giving us a chance to vote
For independence for the Rhu

We'll have a toll bridge at the Braighe
To let the others through
And a ferry sailing daily
Between Bayble and Poolewe
I bet the rest of Lewis
Will have their noses out of joint
When they have to get a visa
If they want to visit Point

Peasdan will be President
To represent our region
After all he is President
Of the Royal British Legion
When entertaining Heads of State
With his medals on his chest
We will sing our National Anthem
Which is come away the reds

The President will have the power
To grant us holidays
On great auspicious days of state
Which fall throughout the year
Every time we win a cup
A day to celebrate
And every time we win the league
A fortnight for a break

The police will be based in Knock
And the firemen at Seaview
Sheshader is ripe for growth
As is Portvoller too
We will have the banks
Way down in Aird
Where they have a bob or two

Down in Portnaguran
In a castle by the shore
In residence Ambassadors
From Lionel to Cromore
In Tiumpan stays the President
And who could ask for more
In Broker in a brand new house
The attaché from Achmore

The Union Jack will fly no more
We will raise instead
The standard of our forefathers
Which is the colour red
That is my utopia I hope my dreams come true
Come and sing our anthem
Which is come away the Rhu

Willie John 'Teddy' Campbell